The Cincinnati Anthology

The Cincinnati Anthology
Rust Belt Chic Press

Printed in the United States of America
First Printing 2014

Book design by Chris Glass
Photo of Bellevue Hill Park by Zan McQuade

ISBN: 978-0-9859441-2-4

www.beltmag.com

The Cincinnati Anthology

Edited by Zan McQuade

Contents

To the People of Cincinnati

Nestled deep within one of the wings of the Cincinnati Museum Center in Union Terminal, just off of the glowing sunrise of the lobby's deco dome, is a miniature model of Cincinnati, a moving diorama of the city through various points in its history. The first time I visited, I fell hopelessly in love with the scaled model, its moving parts, the winding pathways and plexiglass windows through which you could spy on the lives of the miniature city below: Crosley Field, the Zoo, Music Hall. I watched as the lights suspended over the city took it from day—with delivery trucks dashing through city streets past warehouses and shops with striped awnings—to night—with windows of the Italianate houses high on the hills glowing golden above the slow lumbering shift of the long-gone trolleys up the Mt. Adams incline. I knew that I could stay on the other side of that plexiglass forever, imagining the stories behind each lit window, wondering how those streets may have changed since the model was built, how the people who lived there have changed, what parts of Cincinnati's history were preserved by the model, what stories could be imagined in its future.

Wouldn't it be a great thing to try to gather these stories in one place, I thought, to bind them together and send them out into the world for everyone to see? To consider Cincinnati for what existed beyond its stereotype, behind those windows, as a collection of experiences, both good and bad? Wouldn't that be a thing.

I moved to Cincinnati for the first time in 2011 (I grew up just north of the city, but hardly knew it then, and spent most of my adult life on the east coast), lured here by what I can only describe as the thrum of the city rumbling under the hills, the exciting energy of progress bubbling up from the river basin. I could feel that something was happening here, something I could be a part of; it was what everyone was talking about. I saw a city full of potential and ideas; everyone I met seemed to have a full-time job and a full-time passion project. What was happening was the revitalization of downtown and Over-the-Rhine, restaurants blossoming across the city, breweries and flea markets and music festivals, contentious construction projects and neighborhood battles. I had landed in the midst of a sort of Renaissance, a seismic shift, and I wanted to pin something of this feeling down, etch it into the city's collective memory, preserving some of what inspired me to move here in the first place.

That is my intent here with the gathered pages you now hold in your hands: to preserve, to etch, to pin.

Much of what you will see in these pages represents the visions of those who have fallen madly in love with the city of Cincinnati, either for the first time or all over again. These are the stories belonging to some of the city's most legendary citizens, many of those who have passed through one way or another, and many of those who are here to stay. These are the sights of the city that take our breath away: the bridges, the architecture, the ghost signs, the hills, the people we pass on the street corner. These are stories and images both of transition and of immutable sentiments.

The essays in these pages aren't all love letters; each of us can acknowledge that there are faults and cracks in the facade of this city, some that run deep: vast swaths of vacant buildings that could do with saving, hills that need shoring up, lingering racial and neighborhood tensions that need to be massaged out with a more progressive dialogue. An anthology purporting to represent an entire city would not be a fair assembly of ideas if it didn't include criticism, or if it didn't highlight the more challenging parts of living here. I hope that while we're sitting here in Cincinnati on the precipice of great things, we won't neglect to consider that every city is born of change, and that we must consider what change is still necessary to make this city as great as we want it to be.

To tell the story of Cincinnati—a story of every life lived here, of every sight seen—would take more than a handful of essays and photographs, but I hope this anthology will serve as a miniature glimpse of some of the great thoughts this city brings about in us, some of the stories it has created through its past and its present. This beautiful and sometimes troubled city that fosters creative endeavors, that makes us acknowledge race and gentrification, that makes us ponder the view of sky and bridge and brick wall and cobbled street, this city that makes us stop and look around at what's being built and what's being destroyed, at what potential might be around the corner: this is a great and unique city, and this anthology is a window through which you might view the collective greatness that this city can inspire.

Zan McQuade
February 2014

This book would not have happened were it not for the generous logistical assistance and recommendations from the following people: Kevin Fanning, Chris Glass, Emily Gould, Jeffrey Harrison, Robert Hitt, Amy Hunter, Jonathan McQuade, Meredith Melragon, Alison Momeyer, Sridhar Pappu, Randy Simes, Curtis Sittenfeld, Jay Stowe, Linda Vaccariello, and, of course, Anne Trubek and the Rust Belt Chic Press.

Let's start with a story.

Geology is Destiny

Polk Laffoon IV

Polk
Laffoon IV

Geology is Destiny

Sometimes, when I'm driving into Cincinnati from Dayton, I watch the horizon line to the south and feel that quickening of the senses that coming home can impart. The land stretches across the woods and fields (and behind the housing tracts and shopping malls) into a gentle upward slope until the sky claims it, and just when it looks like nothing could lie beyond, the hills come into view again. Gentle, rolling, densely wooded and, in their way, welcoming. When I see them, I know I'm back.

First it's the hills bordering the Mill Creek Valley, far enough apart that their prominence is not immediately apparent. Then, as the city comes closer, the rear slopes of Clifton and Fairview Heights push in from the left; College Hill, Fairmount, and Price Hill loom to the right; and in time, the mounded skyline of Kentucky rises up. Downtown, steeper hills surround the basin. If I am crossing Ft. Washington Way, I glimpse the hill between Third and Fourth streets that local historian Dan Hurley tells me "is the most important of all, because it prevents the city from flooding."

Many of our neighborhoods—Mt. Airy, Bond Hill, College Hill, Kennedy Heights, Mt. Lookout, Mt. Washington, Pleasant Ridge, and Winton Hills, to name a few—take their names from their elevations. Many of our parks—Ault, Alms, Eden, Jackson Hill, Mt. Echo, and Mt. Storm—get their character from their views. Our hills provide pedestals for some of our most familiar landmarks: Holy Cross-Immaculata Church on Mt. Adams, Hughes Center High School in Clifton Heights, St. Francis de Sales in Walnut Hills (the visibility of its steeple from long distances is remarkable), the Twin Towers retirement community in College Hill.

Our hills, the defining feature of our surroundings, are lovely. Naturalist John Tallmadge, in *The Cincinnati Arch*, his homage to the wildness that persists within the city's borders, explains: "Thanks to the Ice Age, we enjoy a steep, complex topography that favors wildlife and confounds the builders . . . Our urban forests come in all shapes and sizes, from large preserves like Mt. Airy Forest or Spring Grove Cemetery (733 acres, half of them wild) to neighborhood parks and backyard borders. Many of these are connected by corridors of varying width from a single hedgerow to hillsides a quarter mile across. Individually, they're as crooked and edgy as jigsaw puzzle pieces. From the air, they make Cincinnati look like a Persian rug, with the colorful, miniaturized forms of buildings and roads woven into an intricate green background."

One day last winter, I arranged to meet Tallmadge. Formerly a professor of literature, currently a freelance writer and editor with a focus on environmental issues, he was quick to elaborate on his prose. "The hills enable wild areas to exist all through the city," he pointed out. "As a result, Cincinnati has animals and greenery that other cities don't have. Moreover, they demarcate the neighborhoods. While it's not entirely true that each is separated from the others by hills, many are. They divide the city geographically, and to some extent socially and economically. In a very real sense, the hills give Cincinnati its character."

Not everyone has shared that reverence. Although early renderings show the hills around the basin as green and wooded, they did not remain so for long. In the public library, the famous Fontayne & Porter daguerreotype of the riverfront in 1848 shows those same hills starkly denuded. Between 1840 and 1870 Cincinnati's population grew from 46,338 to 216,239, and the hillsides fell victim to the pressure. In his 2002 master's thesis, "Land Use and Land Sliding in Price Hill," local geologist and real estate broker Tim Agnello ticked off the mid-nineteenth century abuses: homesteading, road-building, clear-cutting for lumber, livestock grazing, and extensive quarrying. "Look at the plat maps for the hillsides," Agnello said to me recently. "There are paper streets"—streets now grown over and/or planned but not built—"everywhere, and foundations and ruins all over the city. We've got these hillsides for one reason. They're hard to build on. If they weren't, there'd be houses all over."

John Cleves Symmes, the original landholder for this entire region, chose to ignore the hills as he set about selling his acreage. In 1788, he advertised the land between the two Miami rivers as "having excellent soil and climate, an absence of mountains, level country . . ." Less than a century later, state geologist Edward Orton was more realistic. The colluvial slopes of Cincinnati, he wrote in an 1873 survey, would be a "disadvantage" for building. He predicted: "These shales have scarcely tenacity enough to hold their place in steep descents when acted on by water and ice; still less when they have been removed from their original beds can they be made to cohere; and they form treacherous foundations for buildings erected on them or for roadways constructed in them."

Rarely, perhaps, was a state official more prescient. This year's mudslides in Mt. Auburn, along Columbia Parkway, and in Price Hill are only the latest in a long and frustrating struggle between the forces of growth and the forces of gravity. When the debacle on Elberon Avenue burst forth in

January, Richard Pohana, the geotechnical engineer for the city, arrived early one morning to see the earth move "probably 50 feet in two hours." It was a remarkable sight, of course. But for Pohana, who has been keeping an eye on the city's hillsides for 24 years, it was déjà vu.

I have always loved our hills. I can remember, as a reporter for *The Cincinnati Post* in the early 1970s, driving north on Hamilton Avenue and feeling slightly sickened at the sight of the new Ashtree Shopping Center freshly carved from the slope on the west side of the road (today, the complex has been taken over by the Greater New Bethlehem Temple Apostolic Church). The raw cut behind the low-slung buildings spoke volumes: The shopping center didn't belong there. Heavy equipment was able to put it there. No regulations existed to stop it.

Things are better now. We have the nonprofit Hillside Trust, dedicated to the preservation of our hills and views. There are some regulations. There is awareness of the importance of the natural environment and the domino-like consequences of playing fast and loose with it. Still, it never hurts to be reminded.

Drive around the city and look—really look—at the hillsides. Ask yourself: Whose sensibility is at work here, John Tallmadge's or John Cleves Symmes'? When nature is good to us, and blesses us with plenty, our default behavior is to take it for granted. Too often, we abuse it. Here's a cautionary thought that's not entirely irrelevant: The last passenger pigeon died in the Cincinnati Zoo in 1914.

In the Geier Collections and Research Center on West Fifth Street—the building with sculptures of wooly mammoths in front—Brenda Hunda has her office. Hunda is young, with dark hair, bright eyes, and small features. She is intense. The curator of invertebrate paleontology at Cincinnati Museum Center, she lectures frequently, talks rapidly, and on the day I met with her, dropped her professional facade long enough to remark: "I love landslides because they're part of the earth doing what it's supposed to do. The earth's job is to take areas that are high and bring them low. We take risks in accessing some of those areas, but when things happen, it's part of the natural process. Geology is not something that just happened in the past. It happens all the time."

I asked Hunda how our hills were created. The answer was complex, involving an ancient sea that covered Southwest Ohio 450 million years ago; a "super-continent" called Pangea, which, when formed, thrust to the surface the Ordovician rock left under the great sea (we see this rock around us today); an ancient river, the Teays, which flowed north through today's Mill Creek Valley about two million years ago; and three periods of "glaciations," the last of them reaching back only 18,000 years.

In laymen's terms, the great sea receded after several hundred million years, most likely related to the forces of plate tectonics and glaciation. Pangea, the super-continent, uplifted and broke apart; for the next 240 million years, this region was a terrestrial environment, exposed to the actions of erosion. This resulted in the Lexington peneplain that now surrounds us—that vast, almost flat land mass to which the horizon lines of all our hills conform. The Teays River, a gigantic stream, cut into the peneplain and gave birth to the two Miami Rivers and the Mill Creek. In doing so, it also began carving our hills.

The three glaciers that followed—and this is the critical part—each bulldozed the earth, pushing before it a pile of ice, rocks, and debris. At its southernmost point, the glacier formed a "moraine"—in effect, a dam pushing the water of the Teays and subsequently forming river valleys (like the modern Mill Creek Valley) into lakes. As the ice melted and the lakes overflowed their banks, the hills that had begun to take shape with the Teays deepened. They grew from roughly 150 feet deep to their current 350 to

400 feet above the Ohio (which is at an elevation of 500 feet).

The soil left on the surface was the clay that became the inspiration for Rookwood Pottery and the scourge of local gardeners. It is no friend to builders, either.

"The clays of the Ordovician ocean are weak," Hunda explains. "The glaciers carved steep slopes through melting and glacial outwash. When you take an inherently weak material and place it on a high slope, it is destabilizing. Then you expose it to water, and the combination makes a beautiful recipe for landslides. Add to that human activity: loading up the hillside with weight it's not able to bear and creating drainage patterns where they shouldn't be . . . it isn't going to work out well."

And indeed, it hasn't. Cincinnati's history of mudslides is long and messy. Twentieth century records include both gargantuan individual slides and miserable periods of multiple slides prompted by unusually wet weather. Thus we had 87 acres near the Riverside Harrison School on the west side displaced in 1926; the first major documented slide on Columbia Parkway in 1933; memorable problems associated with reconstruction of the Waldvogel (Sixth Street) Viaduct in 1950; and due to construction of I-75, displacements near Cincinnati State that cost more than $400,000 to remedy in 1956 and 1957. Sixteen years later, construction of I-471 triggered a collapse of lower Mt. Adams from below Oregon Street to the base of the hill.

If slide activity is severe enough, as it was in 1973, 1996, and this year, the area affected can qualify for Federal Emergency Management Agency (FEMA) assistance, which means the federal government will handle 75 percent of the clean-up cost. Ohio Emergency Management handles another 12.5 percent, and the city picks up the remainder. Between 1973 and 1978, Hamilton County devoted a total of $31 million to mudslide remediation—excluding the $30 million, give or take, required to shore up Mt. Adams. In 1996, damages from landslides in Hamilton County exceeded $10 million.

Near Richard Pohana's City Hall office is a fascinating city map. The areas prone to serious slides are inked in red—so many of them, they look like flames on the brink of a conflagration. But Pohana doesn't see it like that. "We have come a long way since the 1970s; other cities are just catching up to where we are now," he says. "Most of the roads that should be reinforced on the downside against erosion are." The city now has 1,837 retaining walls holding back the earth. Joined together, they'd make a bulwark 59 miles long.

Arguably, the most significant year in the history of Cincinnati landslides was 1973. In addition to a section of Mt. Adams giving way, major slides occurred along Columbia Parkway, the bend in Clifton Avenue, and on Hillside Avenue in Delhi Township. The combined disasters led to the passage of a 1974 cut-and-fill ordinance mandating that anyone wishing to build on the hillsides submit the plan to the city's zoning department—a measure that environmental activists had lobbied for for years.

Pohana cites one of the most notorious pre-ordinance problems: The Fay Apartments, built in the early 1960s atop one of the southernmost hills lining the Mill Creek Valley, a public housing project commandeered by the United States Department of House and Urban Development (HUD) at a time when no one was thinking about ecology. Builders flattened the top of the hill, poured the sediment over the sides, and slapped down the cheap units that remain an eyesore to this day. "There were no regulations," Pohana said recently. "They overloaded the top, they created draining problems that still persist, and we've been cleaning up ever since."

The second significant milestone in the effort to remediate landslides was an agreement in 1989—the year Pohana came to City Hall—to earmark funds for landslide repair and the kind of capital improvements that would handle slides before they happened, such as reinforcing retaining walls and inspecting them regularly. Approximately $1 million annually was set aside; recently, with the city's budgetary problems, the sum has dropped to more like $650,000 annually.

Even in its diminished distribution, Pohana notes that the money has made all the difference.

On a warm day in January, I walk through the streambeds and ravines of LaBoiteaux Woods in College Hill with John Tallmadge. Trees surround us as far as the eye can see, brown and leafless in the winter light. Tallmadge wants to show me firsthand the wildness within the city that is the gift of our hills. A surprising amount of it, he says, is not in neighborhood parks but in nature preserves and natural areas such as the north end of Spring Grove Cemetery, where we are headed now.

"Over there," he says, pointing, "that beech is old, and old beech trees indicate an older forest. You can tell by its girth." A self-taught naturalist, Tallmadge is curious about everything he sees. Spotting a small, fossilized rock, he runs his finger across its furrowed surface, utters the scientific name—"bryozoan"—and pockets it. Standing on a long, steep embankment in the middle of the woods, he hypothesizes that it is manmade, perhaps the foundation of an early streetcar line. "We can look it up," he says. "The history is usually available."

That much I know. In Tim Agnello's master thesis is a pre-1930 photograph of Bald Knob, a rock formation at the north end of Price Hill. You can't take a photo of it today: It was used for fill to create the foundation for Union Terminal. At the time of the picture, Bald Knob had something of the presence of Mont Saint-Michel—a rock of castle-like proportions towering in the middle distance behind (and slightly to the right of) the site of the proposed train station. Today, it is a low plateau at best. To create the base that supports the Union Terminal foundation, limestone was removed from Bald Knob. To infill portions of the land surrounding the terminal, its shale was used. In all, approximately 4 million cubic yards of limestone and shale were stripped from the huge rock (with another 2 million taken from other locations to infill the valley in the vicinity of Union Terminal). Depending on your sensibility, it was either a wise use of natural resources or blatant environmental degradation.

I tell the story to Tallmadge with a bit of a too-bad-it-had-to-happen spin, but he is sanguine. "People are going to change landscapes," he says. "It's inevitable. People have been here for 200 years. There are more of us than ever, and that isn't going to change." We are hiking now beneath a power line that runs the length of the county; the ground beneath us is grassy, the space open. We crest a hill above Gray Road, look southeast across the Mill Creek Valley, and there, in the distance, are the high-rises of East Walnut Hills and Hyde Park, the towers of the University of Cincinnati and, sure enough, the St. Francis de Sales steeple. Behind us, for a considerable trek, it's all woods and steep descents.

"Sometime," says Tallmadge, "I'd like to hike the whole length of this power line. There's so much to see." He grows excited; his enthusiasm is expressed in decibels. "*Think* of it! We have four places in Cincinnati where you can see old growth trees. Very few cities can say that. It's *amazing*!"*

What is more amazing, I think, is that despite all the people and the urban pressures, and all the damage we have done to them, our hillsides remain magnificent. I recall the previous week, when I stood on the observation deck of Carew Tower with Dan Hurley and looked at the panorama to the north. The thickets of bare-limbed trees and the endless brick buildings

{ **California Woods, Winton Woods, Caldwell Preserve, and Ault Park all contain stands of old-growth forest.* }

rippled across the ridges like a topographical map come to life.

While we were there, Hurley cited the locations of the five inclines, built in the late 1800s and dismantled before the mid-1900s. He pinpointed the pathetic remains of Bald Knob. He nodded toward the Mill Creek Valley, reminding me that it was the only natural way to access the city from the north until I-71 was cut into the shale some 50 years ago.

I listened, and I learned, but mostly I looked. In this city where we can be so preoccupied with river views, I wasn't seeing a drop of water. I was fixated on the hills.

Originally published in the May 2012 issue of *Cincinnati Magazine* as Part One of a three-part essay on Cincinnati's unique triad: its river, its architecture, and its hills.

Love Letter to Cincinnati

David Falk

David
Falk

Love Letter To Cincinnati

Italianate: an architectural style familiar to Cincinnatians, to me, this word means history; it means culture and the effect of row after row of rooftops overlooking the city I have called my home for so many years now. In the mid-nineteenth century, you were the third largest city in America, teeming with breweries, meatpacking plants, and soapmaking facilities; yarn-spinners, potters, drunks, millionaires, future presidents, and every kind of immigrant imaginable. This is the kind of city I wanted to find when I left for New York, Chicago and later Rome. I wanted to be among the romantics, the artists, the students of the good life. I spent ten years searching for something I found almost immediately upon returning. Sometimes moving forward requires going back.

I am a chef. I am a restaurateur. It's what I do and I love doing it. I believe the same things that make a great restaurant make a great city: the connection between a vision and the people who carry it out, the structures that seem to rise from the mind to the sky and the progress of those who create them. Cincinnati, you are a city of creators. Restaurants, like cities, would not exist without the tireless ones, the ones who spend every ounce of energy toiling to make them great because they believe in the vision of visionaries.

I left because I was young and bored. Bored of mediocrity, bored of sugar in tomato sauce, bored of preppy girls with perfectly-starched preppy collars. That's all changed now. You're no longer drinking your pains away with Dayton, making subtle jabs at Akron, when Lebron James was just a glimmer in Cleveland's eye.

Cincinnati, you've grown into yourself, you eat vitamins, you've visited places, famous places, where tourists take photographs. The braces are gone, you learned about "product," people are calling you. They want something long-term.

Yet, you contradict yourself, and damn, if that doesn't make you hot. Your soul contains multitudes, as Whitman put it. You are Findlay Market, teeming with suburbanites and urbanites, homeless and renters, bleary-eyed bachelors and bright-faced families. You are the Roebling Bridge, the singing bridge. Hit me if this sounds lame, but you are hip. You're taking less time to do your nails because you can't wait to get back to killing it.

I don't always love you in winter. Would it kill you to snow once in awhile? But sometimes you relent, covering my Prospect Hill in white and my mind leaps continents and eras to snow-bound villages of my childhood daydreams. I love you in the fall when I drive out to New Richmond and you glow all shades of red, yellow and orange. Spring reminds me why we got involved in the first place: it was a warm sunny afternoon in one of your parks or some tree-lined street, the colors in the sky matching the pinkish hue of your lips. I even love you in summer . . . for about a week, and then the air gets so thick you could swear you were swimming in it. All of your faces are flawed and beautiful and inspire in me the passion I felt when I first saw your skyline stretched over the river as I drove through the Cut-in-the-Hill.

I left you for other women. They did not have your warmth, your endless gratitude or that look you give me when you're ready to leave a party. I remember that I have to share you now—you're a hot commodity, the bee's knees. But you taught me humility. The bend in the river always reminds me of the smiles of my guests as they leave my restaurants. I smile back knowing that sometimes a smile says enough.

When I left, Cincinnati's food scene was largely uninspired. Although, I must admit, I've always been intoxicated by your controversial chili. This strange Greek concoction maligned by some, fiercely defended by others, nursed me through so many hangovers (and contributed to a few). But you've changed and you're so much more. The facsimile boredom has imploded leaving in its white-bread dust gloriously reformed Cincinnati cuisine. You've given hillbillies and debutants equal opportunity to expand a passion for food that would make Fernand Point scream, "Le Grande Cuisine!"

I'm humbled. You've accepted me with open arms, embracing my many quirks and whims, supporting my ambition and allowing me to take root in your core where the iconic Maisonette once held your heart. Shepherding me back to the place where I began. We are lucky enough to have people in this city driven by the pursuit of an ideal; dedicated to doing things the right way, the slow way. There was a time when you couldn't even get a decent cup of coffee in this town. Now, I can't throw a rock without hitting some hipster with a pour-over or a Chemex, but I find it increasingly difficult to start my day without a cup brewed from this "collective" passion for coffee. When I buy beef—aged by generations of butchers—or slide my tongue over cold French Pot ice cream to escape your summers, I feel close to you.

It's true, you're no longer known as the "Crown Jewel of the West," bragging to St. Louis about having the second tallest building in the world, your river filled to capacity with boats and barges, but you rumble with a new greatness. I can feel it when the symphony is warming up to Sheherazade in Music Hall, a building that can stir romance in the most cold-hearted soul; that feeling of butterflies in my stomach like it's the first date. I start to see our future together, imagining what our lives will look like. Will we continue to grow together? Will you always look this good?

Cincinnati, you and I both grew and changed while I was away. You are courageous; a romantic pioneer. I think I realized just how far you had come one night this summer, our city park ablaze with lights, lights that took an army of tech engineers to achieve, lights as a gift to your many lovers, 35,000 of them squeezed together in celebration. To steal a phrase from Fitzgerald's *The Great Gatsby*, in those lights I saw our "orgiastic future." While Fitzgerald's light recedes farther and farther out of view, your light, Cincinnati, shines even brighter. You are no longer that embarrassing girlfriend I don't tell my friends about, insecure and self-conscious. You're alive and breathing in gasps of energy and I scream my love for you from the Italianate rooftops.

Originally published in *The Huffington Post* on October 23, 2013.

Spans

Nick Dewald

Over-the-Rhine

Sarah Wesseler

Sarah
Wessler

Over-the-Rhine

I have spent the past four years being priced out of some of the fastest-gentrifying areas of the United States: traditionally African-American and West Indian neighborhoods in Brooklyn that have witnessed an improbably fast sweep of young, relatively well-heeled, mostly white and Asian people—people like myself—moving in and transforming bodegas into artisanal mayonnaise shops.

Despite my intimate familiarity with the gentrification process, however, when I visit my hometown of Cincinnati I'm always taken aback by the extremes of race and class on display in one of the city's fastest-changing neighborhoods, Over-the-Rhine. Located directly adjacent to the city's central business district, OTR, as it is often called, offers a somewhat surreal refresher in the architectural, economic, and racial history of American cities. On one block, rows of boarded-up buildings abut a tidy, suburban-style townhouse serving homeless veterans, while a renovated single-family row house a few streets away is on offer for $650,000. Ground-level retail in the storefronts of ornate nineteenth-century structures ranges from a men's clothing store covered with jaunty hand-painted signs advertising check-cashing services to a design shop selling $125 tote bags. Representative street life on a snowy winter afternoon: a bored-looking young white valet waiting for customers outside of a just-opened, design-magazine-ready Japanese restaurant; a twenty-something black woman with platinum blond hair proclaiming to no one in particular, loudly and at length, that she had never sold her body and was offended by suggestions to the contrary; a group of black teenagers laughing and joking around on the sidewalk; a well-dressed young white woman walking her dog down an otherwise deserted alley where expensive cars sat parked next to abandoned buildings.

Over-the-Rhine first came to the attention of the world outside Cincinnati in 2001, when one of the largest riots in recent U.S. history broke out there. When I set out to write something about my hometown, I asked myself whether it was worth covering a neighborhood that had already been explored by *The New York Times*, *The Guardian*, MSNBC, and countless others. After all, Cincinnati is a relatively unknown commodity outside of Ohio, and, like any other city, is filled with countless fascinating stories and characters. But there is something special about Over-the-Rhine—something that has inspired both fear and romanticization for decades—and I wanted to understand more about the dramatic changes that are taking place there. It's stunningly beautiful, its history is stunningly tragic, and it serves as a case study of many of the most pressing issues facing cities today: inequality, poverty, gentrification, densification, and privatization.

Cincinnati's founders settled on the northern bank of the Ohio River in 1788. In 1837, the Miami and Erie Canal, which connected the city to New York and New Orleans, was completed at what was then its northernmost border. In the same period Germans began to immigrate to the city in large numbers, giving Cincinnati a Teutonic character that it retains today. When many of them settled just north of the canal, it began to be known as the Rhine, and the land above it Over-the-Rhine. By 1850 a thriving Over-the-Rhine housed a heterogeneous mix of Cincinnati's Germanic population, with prosperous merchants living steps away from poor laborers.

But over the next few decades the demographics began to change. Across the nation, technological advances in transportation and infrastructure and a growth of anti-urban sentiment were beginning to draw those who could afford to leave the city centers. "Suburbia, pure and unfettered and bathed by sunlight and fresh air," wrote Kenneth T. Jackson of this period in *Crabgrass Frontier: The Suburbanization of the United States*, "offered the exciting prospect that disorder, prostitution, and mayhem could be kept at a distance, far away in the festering metropolis." In Cincinnati, the leading citizens began to leave the city's basin and build mansions in the surrounding hills.

Over-the-Rhine became poorer and friskier. "It is the most densely populated portion of the city, and is inhabited by about 25,000 persons, almost exclusively Germans, and Americans of German descent," noted 1880's *King's Pocket-Book of Cincinnati*. "Innumerable variety shows, beer-gardens, and other places of amusement and recreation are in its precincts. It is a famous place of resort at all times, but especially on Sunday, for those who love excitement and beer." By the turn of the century, the population had reached its all-time peak of approximately 45,000.

Over the next few decades, the area's physical and social infrastructure steadily declined and residents left in search of better conditions. Among other factors, the allure of the suburbs was strengthened by the rise of car culture and, eventually, New Deal programs promoting home ownership and encouraging economically and ethnically homogenous communities.

These policies also ensured that Over-the-Rhine would remain a white neighborhood well into the twentieth century. For years the Cincinnati Board of Realtors actively supported the theory that racially similar neighborhoods were best by refusing to help blacks move into white areas, according to Zane Miller and Bruce Tucker's 1998 book *Changing Plans for America's Inner Cities: Cincinnati's Over-the-Rhine and Twentieth-Century Urbanism*. As a result, although several surrounding neighborhoods were predominately black, Over-the-Rhine gradually became filled with poor, white Appalachians.

By 1960, the neighborhood's population had fallen to 30,000. Over the next ten years, the number was halved. By this time segregationist housing policies had fallen out of favor, and for the first time a significant proportion of residents were black. Many of the newcomers had been displaced from the nearby West End neighborhood, which was torn down as part of a slum clearance program.

In the 1970s, decades-old debates about what should be done to improve the neighborhood grew more contentious, evolving into a Hollywood-style struggle between two charismatic young protagonists, Jim Tarbell and Buddy Gray. Tarbell, a restaurateur and future politician who had brought Captain Beefheart and the Grateful Dead to Cincinnati as a rock promoter in the '60s, wanted to lure the middle class back to Over-the-Rhine. Gray, a social worker who dedicated his life to the neighborhood's poor, believed that securing the rights of existing residents had to come first.

Focusing primarily on the issue of housing, Gray and his fellow activists succeeded in limiting market-rate development and establishing control over many existing buildings. However, as time went on, the gulf between the different visions for the neighborhood became ever more entrenched, with the pro-development camp (headed by the Tarbell-founded Over-the-Rhine Chamber of Commerce and Over-the-Rhine Foundation) and low-income resident advocates (the Over-the-Rhine People's Movement, comprising advocacy groups and institutions serving the neighborhood's marginalized residents) competing for the city government's attention and support. "For a long time, it was a battle between the poor people wanting to keep the neighborhood, and other people wanting to take it from them and gentrify it," Elizabeth Brown, executive director of Cincinnati nonprofit Housing Opportunities Made Equal (HOME), told me. "It was this utter battle back and forth, fought in terms of absolutes."

By 1990, the neighborhood's population had fallen to 9,752. The median household income was only $5,000. A quarter of the housing units sat empty; only three percent were owner-occupied. Seventy-one percent of residents were black.

A decade later, the population had shrunk to 7,638. The neighborhood was notorious for crime, drugs, and homelessness. A social worker who lived and worked in Over-the-Rhine in the '90s and early 2000s (and who asked to remain anonymous) told me that neighborhood children had virtually no chance of a normal life during this period. "There's kids I watched, I knew them when they were five years old and I lived there long enough to know them till they were teenagers. These kids had shit for opportunity. They were fucked just by where they were born," he said, the emotion in his voice apparent. "I've spent time all over the country, I've worked around inner-city kids and have spent a lot of time talking to people who did the same thing . . . Over-the-Rhine is an ugly fucking place when it really gets down to it. It is gritty and nasty . . . You're talking about open-air drug dealing on multiple corners. People from other major cities would come to my house, drive down the street on the way to my house where there would be guys just selling drugs on both corners, openly, and they would be like, 'What the fuck is going on? This hasn't happened in fill-in-the-blank-major-city in a decade.' So yeah, you grow up there, you're fucked! No question."

Recent studies have ranked the Cincinnati metro area as America's eleventh most segregated by income (tied with Kansas City and Washington, D.C.) and tenth most segregated by race. While I was surprised to learn about my hometown's national clout in these matters, the segregation itself was not news.

In early 2001, a discussion between business, civic, and political leaders organized by the city's main newspaper reached a grim consensus about the state of black/white relations in the city. Then-mayor Charlie Luken named the issue the city's top challenge. Businessman and community leader Clifford A. Bailey was quoted as saying, "I see Cincinnati as being in denial that there is a race problem . . . The African American community doesn't feel the police are protecting or serving it at all."

A few months later these tensions were thrust into the global spotlight when the city played host to the nation's largest riots since Los Angeles exploded in 1992. As in LA, Cincinnati's were triggered by policing issues. On April 7, a nineteen-year-old African American was shot to death in an Over-the-Rhine alley by a white police officer only a few years older. Timothy Thomas, who was unarmed at the time of his death, was the fifteenth black man killed by the Cincinnati police within a five-year period. During this time, no whites died as a result of police activity. Protests over the shooting and the legacy of entrenched inequalities it pointed to soon gave way to violence and looting. Although there were incidents in several areas, the epicenter was Over-the-Rhine. For days, sensational images of the neighborhood flashed across the world: fires; streets blocked by lines of police in riot gear; dazed victims of both police- and rioter-induced violence; crowds running to escape tear gas sprayings; handwritten signs reading "Tired of talking—stop killing (us) or else!"

These tensions felt a world away when I was growing up, although I was only a twenty-minute drive from Over-the-Rhine. My teens were spent in Anderson Township, a fairly typical outer-ring Cincinnati suburb due east of downtown. Its main corridor, Beechmont Avenue, is flanked by big-box stores, chain restaurants, and strip malls. A turn down almost any side street puts you on a winding, wooded road lined with schools, churches, and subdivisions occupying various positions on the continuum from modest '50s ranch to 2012 McMansion on golf course. Most of Anderson's 45,000 residents live in single-family, owner-occupied houses surrounded by tidy yards; renting seemed exotic and sad to my childhood self. According to the 2010 census, the community is ninety-five percent white, with a median household income of about $70,000. Ninety-seven percent of residents live above the poverty line.

I spent as little time in Anderson as possible as a teenager. One of my favorite escapes was Kaldi's, a nineteenth-century pharmacy turned into a café and used bookstore in Over-the-Rhine. Kaldi's served as a sort of hub for the arts community that had developed in the neighborhood in the 1980s and '90s. Located in what had become known as the Main Street entertainment district, it was surrounded by bars that were also popular with white, middle-class suburbanites.

After the 2001 riots, business slowed dramatically for these and similar establishments in the area. This was due primarily to an increased perception of Over-the-Rhine as dangerous—a quality associated with the neighborhood for as long as I can remember—but also to a boycott of center-city businesses and entertainment promoted by a number of community groups for several years after the unrest. Although some downtown businesses made it through this period, many, including Kaldi's, closed their doors.

Recently, however, a new wave of development has taken hold, with a number of businesses and condos opening in the southeastern quarter. The new storefronts are independently owned, and most align closely with my consumer preferences. There are good bars, restaurants, and coffee shops, as well as a used bookstore, vintage clothing store, and several art and design shops. The Art Academy of Cincinnati relocated there a few years ago. There's a park and a music venue that gets good touring bands. The renovated apartments are nice. A streetcar is scheduled to open in the next few years. If I were to move back to my hometown, Over-the-Rhine would be at the top of my list of places to live—particularly as it's one of the most pedestrian-friendly neighborhoods in a car-dependent city.

Levels of development activity vary widely across the neighborhood. Some streets remain completely untouched, lined by abandoned buildings. A section that has become known by the real estate agent–sounding term the Gateway District, however, has already gone through several stages of gentrification. "Three or four years ago the Gateway District was gentrifying, and it was primarily done by the hipsters," my brother, who lives in downtown Cincinnati, told me. "They're generally still the ones that work at the places that have sprung up there, but it's certainly become more mainstream now. It's a collection of people in their mid-20s through 30s—corporate people from Procter & Gamble and Kroger that avoided the area until now—that go out there and even live there now."

After the riots, it was obvious that something had to change. From what I've been able to tell, however, there was never much of a debate about what that something should be. Police reform, one of the two main streams of governmental response, was a clear necessity. The other—the physical and social restructuring of Over-the-Rhine—has been more controversial.

To put the matter in context, some background regarding Cincinnati's recent history of decision making regarding urban space is useful. Over the past ten years the government has spent a fortune on faddish large-scale development projects, including a convention center expansion and new stadiums for both the Reds and the Bengals. Economic returns on all three have been far below the exuberant projections ("the Cincinnati [football stadium] deal combined taking on a gargantuan responsibility with setting new records for optimistic forecasting," Stanford economist Roger Noll told *The Wall Street Journal* in 2011). I personally wonder if the public money that went toward the Contemporary Art Center's new Zaha Hadid–designed home, which opened in 2003, might have had a greater impact if it had been spent on smaller-scale, more locally focused arts initiatives. The newest major downtown attraction, a casino located just outside of Over-the-Rhine with an eighty-foot-tall sign and oddly aggressive beige facade, seems tragicomic.

Of course, Cincinnati is not alone in chasing questionable development trends. In an influential 1989 analysis of culture- and consumption-based interurban competition, geographer David Harvey argued that the proliferation of cookie-cutter amenities popping up across the country was a result of a fundamental shift in urban governance. Feeling the impact of deindustrialization, decreased support from central governments, and increased geographical mobility of businesses and money, local governments changed their focus from providing services to citizens to trying to attract cash.

But they found themselves competing against one another for a limited pot of business and consumer dollars. "We here approach a force that puts clear limitations upon the power of specific projects to transform the lot of particular cities," Harvey wrote. "Indeed, to the degree that interurban competition becomes more potent, it will almost certainly operate as an 'external coercive power' over individual cities to bring them closer into line with the discipline and logic of capitalist development. It may even force repetitive and serial reproduction of certain patterns of development (such as the serial reproduction of 'world trade centers' or of new cultural and entertainment centers, of waterfront development, of postmodern shopping malls, and the like)."

Interurban competition and declining resources are issues that Ohio cities understand very well. A 2008 Brookings Institution white paper noted that its job growth was forty-fifth among the fifty states from 1970 to 2005, significantly worse than even neighbors facing the same general challenges. Ohio's metropolitan areas, in particular, fall far below their counterparts across the country in terms of job growth. Population across the state has dropped as sprawl has increased, resulting in a glut of vacant land and abandoned buildings. And adding to the complexity of the challenges facing the state, it simply has more cities than most: Columbus, Cleveland, Cincinnati, Toledo, Akron, Dayton, Canton, and Youngstown are forced to share a dwindling pot of funds. "Ohio's cities simply lack the resources to solve their problems," said a 2010 Brookings paper. "Their loss of population and jobs has rendered them disproportionately poor, starved of the fiscal resources they need to provide decent public services, let alone invest for future growth."

So, like other municipalities facing similar challenges, Cincinnati's government has tried a variety of strategies to attract and retain cash and jobs—including, in the case of Over-the-Rhine, planned gentrification. Trying to imagine the pressure of sitting on City Council in the years immediately following the riots, the appeal of this approach is clear. After watching the neighborhood erupt in flames following decades of bitter debate about who should control it, the fact that the enthusiastic, well-connected pro-development camp was eager to inject money and energy into the neighborhood must have seemed like a no-brainer to many. Letting the low-income advocacy groups dictate the neighborhood's spatial dynamics got us here, the thinking seemed to run: now it's the other side's turn.

And so two years after the riots, the city created the body that has been responsible for much of Over-the-Rhine's restructuring, a private nonprofit called Cincinnati Center City Development Corporation (3CDC) whose board of directors is a who's who of the city's corporate leaders. Its remit extends throughout Over-the-Rhine and two other downtown districts. In an article from the time in Cincinnati's main newspaper, city officials said the impetus behind its creation was a growing recognition that development was not the local government's strong point. As a result, they claimed, Cincinnati was falling behind its neighbors. By handing responsibility for building projects over to professional development deal brokers, the city hoped to increase the overall speed and efficiency of development and secure better terms from developers. "The hope is 3CDC will get us there faster, with fewer lost or stalled projects," said *The Cincinnati Enquirer*. "The goal is to spark new housing, shops, offices and arts north from the riverfront through Over-the-Rhine."

In the decade since, 3CDC has acted in a variety of roles (developer, master developer, asset manager, and lender/fund manager) to implement a 2002 Over-the-Rhine master plan. Its strategy has been to identify discrete chunks of the neighborhood to be developed, then land bank empty buildings and lots to build a critical mass of properties on a block, renovate salvageable existing structures, and build new ones to fill the gaps. To date, it reports restoring over a hundred historic buildings, developing almost five hundred residential units and almost 130,000 square feet of commercial space, and creating streetscape improvements and hundreds of new parking spots. It has also purchased businesses suspected of contributing to crime, such as liquor stores. Last summer it debuted a $48 million renovation of Washington Park, the neighborhood's largest green space.

In researching this article, I found that most people with an opinion about recent developments in the neighborhood tend to recount a version of one of two narratives. One goes something like this. First and foremost, it's high time that someone try something new to reverse its decline. Second, the consistent population decline and emptying out of the building stock over the past few decades has left plenty of space for newcomers and existing residents alike, and the benefits of gentrification—less blight, fewer crimes, more amenities—are good for everyone. The influx of middle – and upper-class households and visitors creates a healthier balance and fits in with the neighborhood's history of different groups arriving in waves. It's fair to move some of Over-the-Rhine's social service agencies out of the neighborhood, as has occurred, since clustering a high proportion of the city's most marginalized residents in one area, as failed policies of the past have done, creates havoc for all concerned.

There's also the issue of changing prevailing notions about the city center. Given the environmental and public health dangers associated with sprawl, this is no small concern. In a city where almost ninety per cent of the metropolitan population lives in the suburbs, stereotypes about center-city crime and danger join forces with a proliferation of outer-belt strip malls, big-box stores, and chain restaurants to ensure that many suburban- and exurbanites rarely venture downtown except for work or game days. Meanwhile, the cultural preference for larger, newer homes with bigger yards continues to push the metro area limits ever outward.

It therefore seems self-evident that it is in the public interest to demonstrate that dense urban living can be not only feasible but desirable. From this perspective, Over-the-Rhine's transformation seems to have been a success. Like several apartment dwellers and business owners I spoke to in the neighborhood, Dan McCabe, a cofounder of music venue MOTR, mentioned his pride at serving as an ambassador to the city. "We often see people for the first time from our suburbs coming to Over-the-Rhine, and MOTR is that introduction for them. It's a lot of fun to be in that position, to represent the neighborhood and its progress."

Although it's too soon to tell whether it will make a difference to the city's footprint, the message is being received. In May 2012, conservative local celebrity Bill Cunningham raved about a recent trip to the neighborhood with his wife on his radio talk show. "A few years ago the odds of Bill Cunningham and Penny Cunningham . . . walking through Over-the-Rhine was zero. Zilch. Kevlar. Wouldn't have happened. Most dangerous zip code in America. Crime. Terrible. Drugs. Prostitution. We walked four or five blocks from Central Parkway north on Vine Street, and I felt as warm as if in my mother's arms . . . We went to three restaurants and they were all packed, with a two-hour wait . . . I'm thinking to myself, "Something right's going on. Maybe I should spend less of my time crapping all over the city of Cincinnati and more time experiencing it." . . . So despite what you may think to the contrary, if you live in [names various rural and exurban areas], think about coming to downtown Cincinnati, north of downtown in Over-the-Rhine . . . and tell me in the days, weeks, months ahead that you're not shocked."

The other common narrative about current developments, while not necessarily diametrically opposed to the one described above—many, including myself, see elements of truth in both—paints a far bleaker picture. At its core, it holds that what's going on amounts to a shuffling around of the poor for the benefit of the rich. As Miami University architecture professor and longtime community activist Thomas Dutton put it in a recent paper, "In Cincinnati and Over-the-Rhine, corporations are building sanitized urban playgrounds for the privileged." It contends that displacement, although hard to measure, has already occurred, brought about both by deliberate actions on the part of the powerful—e.g., successful efforts to move homeless shelters out of the neighborhood—and unplanned but predictable consequences of market forces. It predicts that higher prices (and an accompanying rise in real estate taxes) will drive out low-income residents and the establishments serving them and, over the long run, prevent everyone except for the well-to-do from moving in.

This narrative frequently extends to a criticism of 3CDC, which, although not responsible for all of the new development—small, independent actors have been most heavily involved on Main Street, for example—has become the most prominent face of change in the neighborhood. And while it is hard to feel much ill will toward a lone individual working hard to realize his dream of running a small coffee shop, in an era of overwhelming income inequality many critics have voiced skepticism about the motives of the city's corporate elite, which forms the backbone of 3CDC. (From the "About" page of the organization's website: "Cincinnati is fortunate to have a very strong and engaged base of corporate leadership, led by Procter & Gamble, Macy's and Kroger to name a few. More than 30 corporate leaders make up 3CDC's Board of Directors. The corporate leadership of 3CDC is vital to its existence and its success.")

This skepticism stems largely from the fact that Over-the-Rhine itself is of strategic business interest. A bit of Cincinnati background: in a city of two million that feels in some ways like a small town, the largest corporations have a psychological weight in the community that I have never felt from their New York counterparts while living in that city. A job at global consumer products giant Procter & Gamble, the city's third-largest employer, is widely seen as a ticket to the good life. However, these companies' prominence within Cincinnati notwithstanding, when trying to attract top talent on a national level they are held back by the city's sleepy, conservative reputation.

In this respect, Over-the-Rhine's potential value is clear. As a beautiful, walkable, amenity-filled historic area located directly between the central business core and the university district, the city's second largest employment center, Over-the-Rhine could offer the highly sought-after young professional demographic a taste of the big city at a fraction of the cost of New York or San Francisco. For corporations, then, the time and money donated to run 3CDC's day-to-day operations is a good investment, particularly as the largest source of actual development funding is public money.

The question that many critics have asked is whether it is in the public interest to give corporations that are ultimately responsible only to their stakeholders—most of whom have never set foot in Cincinnati—power to make decisions regarding the city's urban space. Although all of its projects have to go through the city planning commission, there is a strong sense among people I interviewed that if 3CDC wants something to happen, it happens.

Of the two narratives, the first is unquestionably more dominant. Several Cincinnatians I spoke to who don't follow politics told me that they were unaware that there was any controversy surrounding Over-the-Rhine's redevelopment at all. With notable exceptions, the majority of media coverage, both local and national, has centered on the concept of dramatic renaissance and rebirth.

3CDC's vice president of communications, Anastasia Mileham, told me that she felt that critics were overrepresented in the media in relation to their actual numbers. "Certainly I'm biased, but I'd beg to differ that a lot of people are unhappy about it. There are certainly a vocal few who tend to get quoted often in the paper, but I'd say you'd be hard-pressed to find long-term residents of the neighborhood who are law-abiding citizens who are unhappy about the changes. I don't care how poor you are, you don't want to live amongst crime and neglect and deterioration."

Nick Dewald, an architect who founded a successful new flea market modeled on the Brooklyn Flea in Over-the-Rhine, told me that he thinks tension between 3CDC and its critics has declined in recent years.* "The negativity about [3CDC] has kind of reached a low point right now, from what I can hear, just because no one can deny that the neighborhood is in as good a shape as it has been since 1940 or something. I think that's sort of undeniable. I can literally think of people who have actively protested 3CDC

{ **Dewald now works at 3CDC, though at the time he gave this quote, he had no connection to the organization. – Ed.* }

who have sat in a lawn chair watching a concert in Washington Park, which is managed by 3CDC. Because a lot of those people who were complaining about 3CDC also love Over-the-Rhine, and if you love Over-the-Rhine you're going to enjoy the neighborhood, and you kind of can't enjoy the neighborhood without enjoying something that 3CDC is responsible for."

There is evidence to support both narratives. There are still many empty buildings in the area, and crime has gone down (although it remains higher in the sections that redevelopment has not yet touched). However, prices are rising, social service agencies are being moved out (often after contentious, highly public debates), and a number of people familiar with the situation say that they believe poor people are leaving.

Different organizations are trying different strategies to help the low-income population stay in the neighborhood. Local developer The Model Group employs a variety of creative financing tools to build high-quality affordable housing. A pizzeria in the Gateway Quarter functions as a job-training program. Churches and social service organizations continue to offer literacy training, early childhood education, food assistance, and more.

In the early days of redevelopment, however, geographer Jean-Paul Addie found little more than lip service paid to preventing displacement among key neighborhood stakeholders. "In discussing the future of the neighborhood with neighborhood organizations and estate agents," he wrote in his 2006 Miami University master's thesis, "there appeared to be little regard paid to how to regulate gentrification or ensure the sustainability of an economically and culturally mixed community after capital investment and competitive markets were established. Interviewees advocating for market-rate development revealed both an apparent desperation and adherence to neoliberal ideology—that stimulating the real estate market was the key to the future of Over-the-Rhine and that everything else would fall into place once these economic conditions were firmly established."

In the case of 3CDC in particular, several people I spoke with told me that the organization had become more involved with affordable housing in the past few years. "Early on, they wanted to do nothing and they'd veto any type of low-income housing. It was extremely difficult," Elizabeth Brown told me. "It was like, 'Well, we don't do that. If you want to build low-income housing, go build it.' But then they would try to block anything that was going on. That's changed today. I can't say they're enthusiastic or that they've embraced it, but they understand that they have to be a partner in these mixed-income developments and low-income housing."

For a current project, Mercer Commons, 3CDC is working with St. Louis developer McCormack, Baron, and Salazar, a specialist in mixed-income housing, to create a dedicated number of affordable units that will be identical to their market-rate counterparts. It has also worked with Over-the-Rhine Community Housing (OTRCH), a nonprofit with deep roots in the neighborhood's affordable housing advocacy community, on a number of initiatives. "Given how our organization was developed over the last 30 years, we have property strategically located in the neighborhood. For the most part, wherever 3CDC turns, we're either across the street or right next door," said Mary Burke, OTRCH's executive director. "So at some point we have to be invited to the table when development is occurring." Joint projects to date include a market-rate property with several affordable units and a twenty-five-unit apartment building serving homeless people with active addictions. Burke also says that 3CDC has also helped her organization find new ways to generate revenue, something that's becoming increasingly vital as federal support for affordable housing shrinks, by helping it put together favorable deals to sell off properties that the larger group needs to complete its projects.

It remains to be seen whether these and related initiatives will succeed in creating a viable mixed-income community. I asked Colleen McTague, an assistant professor of geography at the University of Cincinnati who has been involved with the neighborhood in various capacities for many years (most recently, while conducting a study of day labor employment agencies there), what she thought current trends pointed to. "Social service agencies being asked to leave, or homeless shelters being relocated, day labor employment agencies moving—it gives you a sense there's some kind of something happening to the under- and unemployed," she told me. She was careful to note that no research specifically on the topic existed, and that there was little likelihood that such research would ever find funding. From an anecdotal perspective, however, "it looks to me that there's less opportunity for the underemployed and unemployed to find housing in Over-the-Rhine," she said. "It appears that way."

"I don't have a problem with there being some nice restaurants in Over-the-Rhine," Justin Jeffre, editor of *Streetvibes*, the newspaper published by the Cincinnati Coalition for the Homeless, told me. "But there should also be affordable places for people to go and shop, affordable places to live, affordable places for people to enjoy themselves."

I asked Tony Romano, organizing director of New York–based nonprofit Right to the City, which focuses on gentrification and displacement, whether he considered what I think of as cultural gentrification—the opening of independent bars, restaurants, coffee shops, and galleries that make neighborhoods attractive to, well, me—a problem in and of itself. He told me that even if their creators and patrons have no intention of disrupting the surrounding community, history shows that these first steps are problematic unless existing residents have some control over the process.

I described the current situation in Over-the-Rhine to Mark Partridge, an Ohio State University professor who specializes in urban poverty and rural/urban relations, and asked what he thought the long-term impact on the poor community would be. "A lot of it is really neighborhood-specific," he said. "It's hard to make general statements, that 'Oh, it does push out low-income people,' or 'it has relatively marginal effects on low- and moderate-income households.' Across our academic literature, we can't pin it down. But, saying that, there's definitely some effect. You are pushing out low-income households, and to the extent that you are, you're just rearranging the deck chairs, so to speak. You're making one area prosperous, but another is then going to have a higher concentration of low-income households that may be associated with various kinds of social needs."

Partridge was skeptical about the claim that gentrification's benefits would trickle down to the neighborhood's low-income residents. "Unless you can link the kind of job opportunities that were created to actually hiring low-income residents, at best it's probably a zero sum. You're just rearranging where the poverty takes place. But on the other hand, if the business community came in and says we can create business opportunities that will also create opportunities for low-income workers, then I could see a win-win for both sides. But if that wasn't explicitly a part of the equation when they were starting the development, it probably just was zero sum."

I asked Justus Uitermark, an assistant professor of sociology at the Netherlands' Erasmus University Rotterdam who studies gentrification, if he could help me locate successful global examples of gentrifying neighborhoods where existing communities have been able to remain more or less intact. His response: good luck. "It is very difficult to resist gentrification once it is fully underway. The most effective way to resist gentrification would actually be to try to reduce its speed and try to create structures that keep people in their place—so for instance, making sure that there's some rent controls in place, making sure that there are good community facilities so that people don't move out of the area, keep pressure on politicians to make sure that new houses are being built for the people who live there, and make the cost of gentrification high by demanding that people who are displaced are given a suitable alternative in the neighborhood. But in the end, if you live in a city where market forces are very strong and where the pressure on land is very high, it's extremely difficult to fully resist gentrification."

When low-income residents leave the neighborhood, their choices about where to go are fairly limited, both by price and by some areas' vocal attempts to keep subsidized housing out. And although Cincinnati is a relatively affordable city, price is still a major consideration for people of limited means.

"We have a lot of people that are either paying huge amounts of their income, to the point where if they pay rent they don't eat for a week," HOME's Elizabeth Brown told me. "Or many are living in a substandard, very low-quality market. We get calls all the time in my office about a variety of housing issues, and some of the descriptions of the substandard conditions are just horrific. But people can't move. They're there because they're only being charged two or three hundred dollars a month and yet falling down on their heads, but they can't afford anything else. And when I talk about substandard housing sometimes, the city takes it as 'Oh, we just need to enforce more.' Well, if you shut down all the substandard housing, you'd have homeless camps all over the city."

The National Law Center for Homelessness and Poverty paints a grim picture of the housing options open to low-income Americans. In no jurisdiction in the country does a full-time job at minimum wage provide enough income for a market-rate one-bedroom. Demand for affordable housing far outweighs supply; only a third of low-income families eligible for housing assistance receive it.

According to the Brookings Institution, between 2000 and 2010 the number of Americans living in poverty rose by 12.3 million, bringing the figure to a record high. The population in extreme-poverty neighborhoods (defined as those where at least forty percent of inhabitants live below the poverty line) also rose during this period.

And in the meantime, neighborhoods from Over-the-Rhine to Crown Heights continue to gentrify. I don't have the answers—but I think we need to be asking a lot more questions.

Originally published in *Satellite Magazine*.

Fear of a
COOPER
BLACK
Planet

Signifier Signified

Maya Drózdz

Quality
Buy •
REFRIGERATORS
LIVING ROOMS.
DINING ROOMS.
WASHERS. DRYERS.
STEREOS.
BED ROOMS.
KITCHEN.
STOVES.
T.V.s
SOMETHING 4 EVERYBODY" &U
OPEN 24 HRS. 7 DAYS
•*Oils*
•*Reggae*
•*Crowns*
•*Beedies*

PAINT OFFICE

6 MONTHS-SAME
AS CASH
OPEN
Grocery
•Produce
•Cigarettes
•Clothing
•Cincinnati

OPEN 7 DAYS A WEEK
MEN & BOYS WEAR
'Buy Sell Trade'
Walk In's
"Welcome"

BEST
1 HOUR
POP
P
A
N
T
S

WINE · WHISKEY
FURNITURE
ACCEPTED

Beware
Of
• Phone
Cards
• Cold Beer + Wine
• Cigars
• Incense
• Books

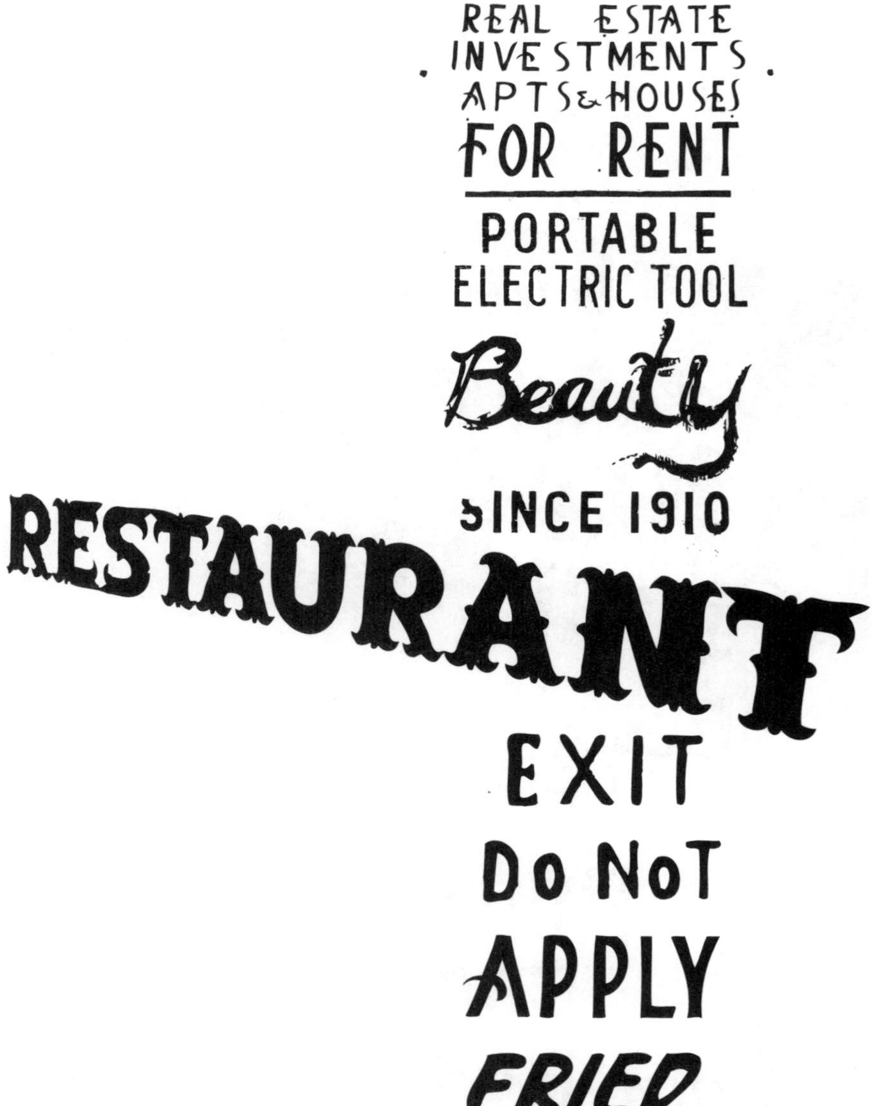
REAL ESTATE
INVESTMENTS
APTS & HOUSES
FOR RENT
PORTABLE
ELECTRIC TOOL
Beauty
SINCE 1910
RESTAURANT
EXIT
DO NOT
APPLY
FRIED
CHICKEN
PAY CHECKS!!

Good'n'Fresh
Household Items
Combined
to Service All
your
CARRY OUT
80-90-100 PROOF
CHILE·SOUPS
& SANDWICHES
much more
flavor

My City in Two Dog Parks

Brian Trapp

Brian
Trapp

My City in Two Dog Parks

With respect to every urban space we should ask ourselves how it functions: for whom, by whom and for what purpose. Are we merely impressed by its sound proportions or does it perhaps also serve to stimulate improved relations between people.

Herman Hertzberger, "The Public Realm"

I live in a neighborhood called Over-the-Rhine, in Cincinnati, Ohio. When I walk my dog, Betts, she mashes her nose into the ground, excavating smells—communicating with the space in a way I cannot. I don't know what information she receives, how far back she can read. Can she smell the dog that walked by an hour ago? The gnawed-on chicken wings dropped

{ *This essay was written and originally published in the fall of 2012. The renovation of Washington Park is now completed, and the author now lives in Northside. – Ed.* }

the night before? The box of moldy clothes that sat there last week? Or can she go back further? Whatever she smells, it must be interesting, because she often tries to rip my arm off for one more whiff.

However, she is a dog, and her knowledge is limited. She certainly can't smell that this used to be a German neighborhood, supported 45,000 people, almost seven times its current population. She is likely unaware of the 300-plus empty buildings, but she's certainly fascinated by the trash strewn across 700 vacant lots. She doesn't know that the buildings she trots under are ancient, the largest collection of nineteenth-century Italianate architecture in the United States, or that they are endangered. She can't smell the ash and blood from the 2001 race riots, which have washed away long ago. Does the odd juxtaposition of businesses mean anything to her? Does she pause to see the strange mix of check cashing centers and yoga studios, corner stores and organic groceries, fried fish establishments and overpriced urban eateries, art galleries and homeless shelters, all in the same few blocks? Unfortunately, she mostly pays attention to food and pee.

For all she doesn't know, she is the medium through which I know my neighborhood. Although I take her for walks, she also walks me, through neighborhood streets, spaces, and people. As much as she's my beloved pet, my dog is also a furry and badly behaved ontological instrument. As I walk my dog through my neighborhood, I see the battle being fought for its future. Will it be a gentrified enclave, a dark ghetto, or a diverse urban village? I don't know, but my dog really has to take a piss.

Northern Row Park

Northern Row Park is not an official dog park, but that's mostly what it's used for. When we approach its cast-iron gate, Betts wheezes against her choker collar to see if another dog is inside. When there is, every muscle in her forty-pound stocky build strains to get closer. She yaps like a psychotic squeeze toy, and on her back forms a stripe of raised, brown fur. She forces her head under the gate, snarling and flashing fangs, and the other owner, someone I haven't met before, looks nervous. He asks, "Is he friendly?" which really means: "Don't let *that* in here" and "Your dog looks like a boy." He winces as I open the gate, and just as my monster is about to rip into the soft of his dog's throat, she stops, sniffs its privates, and wags her tail—a white flag. The owner squints: "What kind of dog is that?"

That is how I meet most of my neighbors. My dog is a slobbering conversation piece. She looks hilarious, a breeding experiment gone wrong. She has the head of a pit bull and the legs of a wiener dog, with a muscled jaw and body atop four stubby legs. I adopted her from the SPCA last year, and to date, she's dug five holes in the carpet, eaten three remote controls, chewed five pairs of shoes, and munched half a string of Christmas lights. The dog she most closely resembles is whatever kind you find in junkyards. "I don't know," I say. "Maybe basset hound and pit bull? Something that shouldn't have mated."

We watch our dogs wrestle around the park's cobbled court and run through the grass and dirt perimeter. I turn to the owner and ask: "You live around here?" It's a dumb question. They always do.

They live on Main and Sycamore, Orchard and Fourteenth Street, in the old tenements that are now rehabbed apartments and condos. They are lawyers and actors, janitors and store owners, PR men and bartenders, students and salespeople. They have lived here fifteen years, five years, six months, a week. They work downtown or in the adjacent neighborhoods, and they mostly have mutts, though there is the occasional purebred.

When their dogs have to take a shit, they come here, one of the only green spaces in the area, if you discount vacant lots.

This is not a public park, not anymore, but they have a right to be here. The park was made not by city planners but by the residents, reclaimed for the community from asphalt-cracked urban decay.

Northern Row Park has existed for as long as anyone can remember. It's named for the northern row of houses on the edge of the city, which used to be at the end of the block on Liberty Street. With the Miami and Erie Canals (now Central Avenue) delineating the neighborhood's southern and western boundaries, and with its substantial German population, the neighborhood was nicknamed: "Over-the-Rhine."

Most of its buildings were constructed between 1865 and the end of World War I, when German-Americans dominated the area. OTR was one of the most densely populated neighborhoods in the country, second only to Manhattan, and in 1900 was home to more than 45,000 people. The neighborhood was bustling and vibrant, but certainly not idyllic, reeking with thick smog from the various industries and stench from the packed-in humanity. With the advent of the automobile, much of the middle class migrated out to the expanding suburbs, leaving OTR's tenements to the working class and poor. In the 1960s, African Americans migrated from the south and from surrounding neighborhoods razed for a new highway. The latter half of the twentieth century follows the tragic plot of every Rust Belt city: investment in the surrounding suburbs and disinvestment in the urban core, leaving the buildings to decay and blight, and the people to fight for city services and quality education from a dwindling tax base. Most of the white residents left, and OTR became predominantly black and poor, with high crime. The population has shrunk to 7,000 in 2010 (36 percent white, 62 percent black, mostly low income).

When John Spencer discovered Northern Row Park in 1990, it mirrored the state of the neighborhood. It had an island of green space in the middle, surrounded by a sea of cracked blacktop, and a rusting swing set from the 1950s that no sane kid would sit on, a teetering death trap. A pair of shoes hung from the telephone wires above, marking the territory for drug dealers. Homeless people used the park as a bathroom. Spencer, a local architect and developer, had just moved into an adjacent building, and with his business and life partner, Ken Cunningham, he aimed to rehabilitate OTR's architecture. He reported the dangerous equipment to the city, but they merely took the swing set away, leaving the space empty. "We decided it could be something," he said. "We could take it over and make it into a park worthy of a new neighborhood."

But nothing gets done quickly in Cincinnati. After seven years in negotiation with the park board, in 2004 they were allowed a ninety-nine-year lease for a pittance. They had just converted their building into condos and the new residents were excited about rehabbing the park as a neighborhood project. Over the course of a year, about forty neighbors worked to transform the park. They wrote grants and raised $100,000, convinced the city to donate old granite pavers from the downtown bus terminal, and did the grunt work. They freed the existing hawthorn and elm trees from asphalt encasements. They dug up drug paraphernalia and railroad irons, and in their place left a natural dirt area on one side and grass and a rose bed on the other. They installed street lamps and flood lights hanging down from the trees, and wrapped the space with a cast-iron fence, punctuated on a diagonal by two gates.

Spencer said he wanted the space to be a "passive area of recreation," as a "nice green space that people could enjoy." People have used the park for neighborhood parties, concerts, movie nights, weddings, chiminea camp fires, picnics and lunches. But to Spencer's mild regret, the space has mostly gone to the dogs: "There is such a need for dog space, it's overrun." The dogs have dug up flowers and trampled the grass into sad clumps. When they're in the park, they dissuade most people from passing through or loitering, and they've left land mines of crap all over the green.

However, as Spencer noted, the dogs signify a strong pulse for the neighborhood, a sign of health. "As you get more people with dogs, it indicates two things: more people with disposable income, and more people meeting each other," he said. "It's a great mixer. That's what is important about living in an urban area: the opportunity to meet and find out about other people."

A dog park is a space to fight against the anonymity of the city, where neighbors are forced to interact in a common space. We have no other tasks to complete. We have nowhere else to go. We must loiter long enough for our dogs to do their business, and even if you're socially awkward like me, you'll eventually interact with the other human being across from you. We get to know each other.

But this knowledge is often limited by and filtered through the dogs. For instance, I know my neighbors value fairness. My dog often plays with a beagle terrier mix named Spence (no relation to John Spencer). His owner, a professional woman of about forty-five, cheers for him as if he's a child playing soccer: "Get her, Spence, get her!" She spends her time clapping. It's hard to have a conversation. But when my dog bites Spence's collar and throws him around, she objects: "Hey, Betsy. Play fair." She separates them like a referee.

"Fair?" I say. "Look where we live. These are street rules." She disagrees.

They also seem to think their dogs' private space should be respected. Several people have bitchy ankle-biters that are not at all friendly. The pugs in particular strike me as hissing, furry lizards, as Betts' attempts at play are met with hard nips from their little fist mouths. One small and black French thing with an actual French name, "Miniot," also snaps at my dog. His owner excuses its aggression: "Say, 'I'm too delicate to play.'" There are dogs too delicate to play.

In addition, I know most of my neighbors don't have kids, because they treat their pets like children. Besides the cheering, they confess to buying soy products at gourmet pet food stores. They have taken their dogs to expensive obedience classes. They often greet the dogs first and the people second. One yuppie couple even named their dogs 'Sophie' and 'Addison,' which are not at all dog names, as if they wanted to practice the names on other living things before they moved to the suburbs and bequeathed them to their children. They cheer, correct and scold. As our dogs tear up the park and slam into one another, they look at me with exasperation, as if to say, "These kids . . . " I too am guilty of this anthropomorphic infantilization. I live alone, and in my weaker moments of existential loneliness, I might vocalize what my dog would be thinking if she had the intelligence of a spunky, eight-year-old child. But let me be clear: Betts eats regular dog food, is hopelessly misbehaved, and though her name is not 'Fido' or 'Ace,' it's still one syllable and not as yuppie-child as 'Sophie' or 'Addison.'

Lastly, I know that we don't necessarily trust one another. People hang plastic grocery bags on the iron fence. This is understandable, as the park can only function if everyone does their part, and if the system of personal responsibility breaks down, things could get pretty crappy. If others aren't playing fair, why should you, and then everyone has poop on their shoes. So the bags are tied around the fence in case you need them, but are also devices of shame, as if your neighbors expected you to not plan ahead, to forget your bag, and are such good people that they make sure you're good too. *Bastards.* You remember your bag next time.

But as much as dog park culture sometimes annoys me, it has also opened my neighborhood. Sometimes, while we watch our dogs fight over sticks, we have genuine conversations. We learn where people used to live and what brought them to the neighborhood. We share intel on favorite restaurants and bars. We learn that the owner of the German shepherd also bikes to work every day, and share stories of car aggression. We learn that the wine salesman is taking a business trip to Argentina, and when he comes back, we ask him how it went. The actors tell us about upcoming productions. We learn that someone's sister is having brain surgery. And, if there's a horrific act of violence in the neighborhood, we have a place to worry and vent. Some of us are even close friends. Some of us kiss when we see each other.

Even if most of these interactions are trivial, they draw us out of private life and make us feel included in the fabric of the neighborhood. It's akin to how urban critic Jane Jacobs characterizes interactions on city sidewalks in *The Death and Life of Great American Cities*:

> *Most of [the contact] is ostensibly trivial but the sum is not trivial at all. The sum of such casual, public contact at the local level [...] is a feeling for the public identity of people, a web of public respect and trust, and a resource in time of personal or neighborhood need.*

While not a city street, the dog park is similarly vital to my public identity. While exercising my dog, I form lasting, if mostly superficial, relationships with the people around me. But those interactions add up into a public identity. I am Betsy's owner. I live on Main Street and ride my bike to work. I am an English teacher and writer. My politics are fairly liberal. I patronize local bars and like good beer. I am thankful that John Spencer and other residents have given me a place to be this public self, have built a space for me and my dog.

But this dog park is also a limited space. As Spencer said, having a dog in the city allows you to "find out about other people," but what kind of other people? Almost all of the dog park attendees are middle class or upper middle class, have no children, and are white, like me. Where is everyone else? If this is Spencer's "new neighborhood," where is the old one?

Data Pit/Pit Data

> If you aint from here, don't come round here.
>
> – *Spray-painted on an OTR building, Thirteenth and Main, September 2010*

When I first moved to the neighborhood, I discovered one of the great OTR dog-walking benefits: you don't need to bring a bag. When your dog pops a squat, the streets are so filthy that, almost without fail, you will have a variety of trash to choose from. Do you luck into a shriveled plastic bag under the curb, or is there a spare White Castle bag overflowing from a trash can? Like the local organic grocery store suggests, I like to reuse and recycle.

But once, when Betts squatted on Fourteenth Street, I couldn't find a piece of trash right away. I panicked. How far could I walk before people think I'm just leaving? Apparently, I passed the boundary. An old lady called down from a third-story window: "Hey! Don't be leaving that shit right on the street! We gotta live here! We *gotta...live...here*!" How could I explain the great dog-walking benefit?

So I shouted back: "I gotta live here too!" I eventually found an appropriate piece of trash and made a great show of cleaning up. But this incident underscores the hostility towards middle-class white people coming in to OTR. For a long time, as Spencer notes, Main Street was primarily an entertainment district for people like me. Young suburbanites and university students would drive in for night life, and the young white people who did rent had more interest in partying than investing in the neighborhood. When this lady saw me and my shitty little dog, she probably assumed that we were invaders who didn't care about the community, about the people who actually "gotta live here."

But this is not the typical reaction I get when I'm walking Betts on the street. At least once on any given walk, I am asked a version of the same question: "What kind of dog is that?" And if they're local black or white working-class residents, they usually have a hunch. Sometimes they just say it: "Dat'a pit." They see the pit bull in the ball of muscle on each side of her head, in her large mouth and Egyptian eyes, in her chest thrown forward and stocky build. But what is up with those legs? "It looks crossed with a wiener dog," they often say, and might be right.

The conversations don't go much farther than that, but sometimes they do. Mostly, they make comments about her physique and praise her leash-pulling power: "She's built. Look at that, long and strong." They might offer advice: "You should mate her with a tiger pit." When she sees another dog walking across the street, lunges against her leash, and squeak-barks, I hear: "Get 'em, killer."

Consequently, sometimes they get the wrong idea about why I have her. Once, when Betts jumped up on a homeless guy and I apologized for her bad behavior, he offered me training advice: "Don't let anyone pet her. You want a guard dog, right?"

"No," I said. "I want a companion dog."

"Okay. Let them pet her, but never as much as you."

In a 1990 study of an unidentified gentrifying urban neighborhood, sociologist Elijah Anderson points out that "within the black community, dogs are used mainly as a means of protection, whereas the middle class whites and blacks in the Village generally see them as pets as well." In other words, if lower-class black and white people have dogs, they often don't see them as fur children. In a poor area with high crime, you need a dog that is aggressive and intimidating, that will convince criminals to move on to the next guy. This is not the kind of dog you want fighting over a stick with a labradoodle.

I'm not saying all lower-class people view their dogs this way. And I'm not saying all of my conversations on the street take on this tenor. Sometimes the conversation will start with my dog's pit-bull strength, but then move on to other topics. One black man I see regularly praised Betts' muscle, but has since taken a liking to her as a pet. He hangs out on a stoop near my building and insists that Betts calls him "Uncle James" while he calls her "princess" and "queen of the block." Sometimes after initial exchanges about my dog, one of us will ask: How you doing? His mother is visiting or his grandkids stopped by. He's been sick all week or he's feeling young and how about this weather? Sometimes we talk about women. Sometimes we talk about changes in the neighborhood. "It's changing much too fast," he said. "I don't like it. A lot of people have moved away." He recently told me that he used to work in demolition and I told him I was a teacher. But what we did for a living didn't seem to matter much. He's the guy who sits on the stoop and I'm the guy who walks his dog. We don't talk about much beyond my dog, but we often say "hi."

Still others on the street act like my dog is public property. I've had all races and classes kneel to my dog without asking and whisper sweet nothings in her ear: "Hi. You're pretty and sweet." Recently, a Hispanic man asked if my dog spoke Spanish, and then proceeded to whisper Latinate as he scratched her ear. I've had a wealthy-looking white man at the farmer's market publicly humiliate himself as he knelt and made out with my dog's head. My canine has a democratizing effect. She is a public object of affection for all.

These interactions on the street are perhaps even more trivial than in Northern Row Park. We are on the move with less time to loiter for sustained conversation. But for feeling part of the neighborhood, the old one not cut off by a cast-iron fence, this contact is much more important. Over-the-Rhine has a terrible reputation. Mention you live here to some Cincinnati suburbanites, and it's as if you've confessed an elaborate plan for suicide. I would be lying if I said OTR's bad reputation doesn't sometimes loom in my mind, especially when it seems confirmed by crime reports and pops of gunfire. I spent my teenage years in a homogenized, upper-middle-class suburb outside Cleveland, with five black people in a high school of 520. With my upbringing, it would be easy to feel threatened.

But Betts provides a reason to interact with anyone on the street. When I'm with her, she forms my public identity. I am not some dorky white guy invading the neighborhood. Foremost, I am the owner of a funny-looking dog. I cannot control who she sniffs or jumps up on, and I cannot control who talks to her. For all her ferociousness with other dogs, she loves people, and is as amiable with the black homeless man who compliments her strength as she is with the white soccer mom who babbles baby talk in her ear (though I hope she likes the homeless man better). A dog can break down the defenses we build to protect us from each other.

But I know she can provide a false sense of security. If threatened, she could take a good chunk out of a perp's leg. She might persuade a criminal hunting for a victim to keep looking. But you're still playing with probability. You think: *if I bring my dog, I will be safe. If I don't sell or buy drugs, I won't get shot. If I don't go on Race Street at night, I won't get robbed.* But the terrifying thing about violence, especially in a poor, urban neighborhood, is its randomness. On my street a few months ago, a pregnant woman was shot during a robbery by a fourteen-year-old kid. Months before that, two innocent women were shot with stray bullets in a failed drug hit inside Tuckers, a diner known for its vegan burgers. My dog, long and strong, will not protect me from desperate kids or stray bullets. But she will have to pee. She will get me into the street and talking pit bulls with people I might otherwise fear. She facilitates the trivial interactions that build trust, that make you less afraid, that give you a place to start a conversation: "What kind of dog is that?"

When my dog pulls me down the street, people often ask: "Who's walking who?" It's a better question than they know.

The Renovation of Washington Park

When planning dog parks, it's tempting to give every interest group exactly what it wants—big dog sections, little dog sections, puppy-only areas, agility courses, natural hiking areas. But, any single dog park cannot be all things to all pooches.

Roxanne Hawn, "Canine Design"

By the time this essay is published, starting in July, when Betts wants to take a piss and fight other dogs, we can walk down Fourteenth Street and keep going, past the boarded-up buildings and rehabbed apartments, past the faded, empty storefronts and sleek, new eateries, and onto a narrow street that leads to a most glorious dog park.

This park will make Northern Row look like a vacant lot. Located inside OTR's Washington Park, this official city dog park will consist of two sections covering a total of 10,000 square feet. Planners have toured dog parks in Chicago and New York, learning from greater metropolises' mistakes and successes, to create a dog park worthy of my city. Unlike Northern Row, there is no risk of an escaped dog every time you open the gate. This park will have a double-gated system with two levels of fence: one buffer area with another layer to enter the play area. Inside the park, we will not tread on shriveled clumps of grass and secondhand pavers, or have to worry about killing the perennials. This park will have specially designed synthetic dog turf that looks like real grass but isn't, with a built-in irrigation system to spray off poop. Unlike Northern Row, where the dogs drink rank rain water from a stone slab, this park will have continually moving water from an artificial creek, where the dogs can drink and play, and if their thirst is not sated, they can wander over to the dual-use people/dog drinking fountain with a built-in bowl at the bottom. There will be large rocks and boulders on which canines can climb and benches on which their owners can sit. Surrounding trees will shade the park from the hot summer sun.

This dog park will be awesome. Betts and I will go here all the time. So why are some people so angry about it? Why would the NAACP lobby city council to deny it taxpayer money? Why would people hold protests to lament its construction? Who are these stone-hearted dog-haters? Do they not like to see puppies frolic?

To understand that, you must understand who lives around Washington Park, and who is moving in. Music Hall lies to the park's west end, housing the Cincinnati Symphony Orchestra and the Cincinnati Opera. It's an imposing, cathedral-like Gothic theater, made of nearly four million red bricks formed in garrets and turrets, with an ornate circular glass window in the center that overlooks the park like an all-seeing eye. In its shadow is the greatest concentration of social services in the city, including the Drop Inn Center, a 250-bed shelter that serves the area's large homeless population. There is also a sizable amount of low-income housing as well as twenty-five vacant properties in the park's immediate vicinity. The area's existing residents are predominantly low-income and black.

However, the area is rapidly transforming. Cincinnati's Center City Development Corporation (3CDC), a private, non-profit firm charged by the city with rehabilitating the urban core, has put more than $162 million into the park and OTR buildings since 2004. Along with my glorious dog park, they will build an interactive water splash ground with more than 400 water jets, a state-of-the-art playground with built-in musical instruments, an artificial stream that pays tribute to OTR's canal history, performance stages with extensive programming, and a "civic lawn" the size of a football field. And in April, directly adjacent to the park, the city broke ground on a streetcar system. With all these improvements to their blighted neighborhood, why would existing residents object to a dog park?

First, it's not a space for them. As I've mentioned, low-income people tend to have dogs for protection rather than as companions, and the city's dog park rules explicitly try to keep those dogs out: "Aggressive dogs are not permitted." But most low-income residents don't own dogs in the first place. As John Spencer mentioned, dog ownership is a sign of disposable income. When you make the neighborhood yearly median income of around $10,000, you will not want to shell out an average of $600 per year for a slobbering freeloader, no matter how cute. What's more, many of the area's landlords forbid pet ownership, because it makes turning over apartments cost-prohibitive. If you're living from paycheck to paycheck, at risk of getting evicted for the slightest financial problem, owning a dog would limit your housing options.

The dog park, as low-income advocates argue, is for the (implicitly white) middle-and upper-middle-class people moving into nearby rehabbed condos and market-price apartments. But what's wrong with that? Shouldn't they have a place for their dogs to run around? Aren't there enough valuable amenities in the park-at-large for lower-income people to enjoy? *Can you say "splash ground"?*

The problem starts when you consider what the dog park will replace. Before 3CDC started renovating, the space reserved for the dog park was formerly a deep-water pool and a basketball court. To the NAACP, this erasure has class and race implications: the basketball and swimming pool are amenities that "poor African American children use" while the dog park is not. According to Josh Spring, executive director of the Cincinnati Homeless Coalition, the residents made it clear that they wanted the pool and courts to stay. In public planning meetings, 3CDC showed pictures from parks around the world and residents were to put a sticker on the one that they liked best. All of the pictures were missing one thing: a pool. He said that someone wrote 'pool' on one of the pictures and at the end of the night, it had "lots of stickers beside it." In addition, students from a local university redrafted the park plans, putting in the pool and courts in place of one of the dog park sections, but this alternative plan was ignored.

I can have some sympathy for the city and 3CDC. As much as the alternative design sounds like a nice compromise for everyone, the minimum space required for a dog park is 8,000 square feet. Crowding can make dogs aggressive, and what if they can't fit in the climbing boulders or artificial creek? In addition, other forces seem to be working against the pool, including low attendance, high cost and neighborhood pool density. And besides, if people want to cool off in the park, they have a ground that splashes, for Christ's sake.

But I find 3CDC to be conveniently ignorant of the class and racial implications of their spaces. Project Manager Chad Munitz denies that that the dog park has a racial or class component: "I can't imagine owning pets and enjoying animals has anything to do with a racial and class system. That's not how we envision the park and not how it will be operated." But owning a pet, especially one that will play nice, is very much dependent on both race and class. Meanwhile, the lack of a basketball court seems particularly pernicious. If you have a "civic lawn" the size of a football field, you could at least put a court in one end zone. If we view Washington Park as the focal point for the neighborhood, then the spaces and how they display the residents are of the utmost importance. As cultural critic Sharon Zukin said, "To ask 'Whose city?' suggests more than a politics of occupation; it also asks who has a right to inhabit the dominant image of the city." 3CDC and the city have decided the dominant image of OTR will not be a poor black man executing a pick-and-roll, but rather a middle-class white guy cheering on his pooch.

Why can't it be both?

There are other issues with the dog park and the park at-large, many of which were hysterically voiced at a protest last year next to the fenced-in construction site. The activists claimed that there was no effort to employ OTR residents in the park's construction. In addition, their local grade school, which was demolished with the promise to build a new one, was replaced with a regional magnet school for performing arts that does not necessarily educate OTR children. Not only were neighborhood people missing out on good paychecks, but their families were moving away to be closer to schools. They also claimed 3CDC is attempting to move the Drop Inn Center, having already convinced another homeless shelter to relocate. Lastly, the 450-car garage being constructed under the park will not serve the residents, but rather outsiders, who will drive in for the school and park, as well as for the area's burgeoning shopping district, which will cater to young professionals. These people will need somewhere safe to put their Kias and Volvos.

The protesters' main concern, and perhaps at the heart of what the dog park portends, is that dirty five-syllable word: gentrification. As sociologist Ruth Glass originally defined the term in 1959, gentrification is the process by which a working-class neighborhood is "invaded by the middle classes—upper and lower," who rehabilitate its buildings and raise its property value, until "all or most of the original working class occupiers are displaced and the social character of the district is changed." Although this definition has been complicated since, it contains the two main elements: physical and cultural displacement. The protesters claim that some displacement has already occurred, as low-income landlords have kicked out residents and sold to 3CDC for condo conversion. But most displacement happens indirectly: as the neighborhood "improves," current residents are priced out of their apartments and homes. As activist Ricardo Taylor said, "They're trying to make it an exclusive neighborhood. People not having the goods aren't going to be able to afford it and will have to move. And they're changing the park to fit someone else's ideals." In this line of thinking, the dog park is perfectly suited for Washington Park, because when the property value goes up, only people who can afford fur children will be able to live there.

I can understand the protesters' ire. While supposedly a neighborhood park, it is mostly designed for people who don't live there yet, and visitors driving in from around the region. And whether it was intentional or not, there are some clear racial and class implications about 3CDC's design and programming choices.

And yet I am freaking excited about this park. I'm looking forward to taking my dog there to scrap with other dogs, and talking to fellow dog owners about new restaurants and bars. I want to put my face in a splash ground water jet, and go to a jazz trio on the "civic lawn." And as much as I hate to say it, I might breathe a little easier when the Drop Inn Center has moved and there's not a loud group of homeless men yelling at one another and taking up all the benches. My enthusiasm makes me wonder: Am I part of the problem? Am I unwittingly paving the way to displace people from their homes?

I fit the profile. As a graduate student and teacher, I am a professional or at least a professional-in-training. I am in my late twenties and have no kids. My apartment, for which I pay the market rate of $700 a month, used to be owned by Tom Denhart, the biggest low-income landlord in the city. At one time, he owned more than one thousand low-income units, but sold out to market-rate developers in the early 2000s, including Urban Sites, my landlord. I am unwittingly guilty of poor-person displacement (Cue foreboding music).

And though I don't make nearly enough money for the typical gentrifier, I do have another kind of worth. As Zukin sees it, gentrification is based on "consumption of cultural capital" and is dependent on "cultural mediators" that "help transform the qualities of a specific place in the built environment into a market for a wide variety of consumer goods." I hold literary readings in OTR bars and invite my friends to eat and drink at its "unique" restaurants. I brag to friends who pay higher rents in other neighborhoods and talk up my "authentic" and "diverse" neighborhood. I walk my dog at midnight, giving the impression that the neighborhood is safe. I spread the word to other middle-class white people that you should come on down, because the water is fine. As a cultural mediator, I am guilty.

Suddenly, Northern Row Park seems much more sinister. The dog park is not a gathering space for community, but rather a gentrification headquarters where we can surround ourselves with people like us, display cultural capital by knowing the hippest restaurants and bars, best beer and newest music. We display our disposable income in the form of our pampered pets, who in some cases are even "too delicate to play." We plot about what "unique" new businesses to support, welcoming the incoming white middle-class hordes, and look forward to the day OTR becomes one giant dog park.

And John Spencer, the benevolent developer who reclaimed my park from urban decay, is really a gentrifier and displacer. His aim may be to rehab OTR's buildings into their authentic and historical character, but, in Zukin's terms, he is also using "authenticity" as a "tool" that "along with economic and political power" is used to "control not just the look but the use of real urban spaces." By converting the unique and historical character of the neighborhood into market commodities for condo owners, Spencer is destroying someone else's city: what makes the neighborhood unique and historical for lower-income African Americans. He said he came to

OTR to "create a neighborhood that was still mixed, that was still 10 to 15 percent low-income." To create this kind of mixed neighborhood, where people can learn from one another, "sounds kind of utopian," he said. But for low-income people, 10 to 15 percent will sound kind of like hell. Their city and the people they know and love would be gone.

When viewed this way, Northern Row Park becomes one more ploy to increase property value, and belongs to a private developer to boot. Every time I take my dog there, I help them. I blaze another path through OTR for middle-and upper-class white people. And who knows how much property value will go up? Is it only a matter of time before I'll be priced out of the neighborhood as well? I can only work so many extra hours at the student writing center. Is John Spencer trying to displace me? I'm a cultural mediator, for Christ's sake. He can't do this to me.

I think I'm freaking out a little. In portraying all development as "rich versus poor," I can highlight important inequalities, but it also bludgeons the city's complexity, making for reductive arguments flavored with paranoia. And John Spencer is a nice guy. He was a mentor to several low-income children before it was popular, helping them with homework and attending after-school activities. For all his development talk, he cares about the old neighborhood and the people in it.

As for my white guilt, it's a little too soon. This neighborhood could use more middle-class white people, and just more people in general. According to census data, the population has dropped to 7,000, an 8 percent decline in the last ten years. The neighborhood's long-term goal is to reach a population of 15,000, and now it's farther away than ever. In addition, people in OTR have been crying gentrification for nearly forty years. As historians note, starting in the 1970s, the city attempted to make Over-the-Rhine "a chic neighborhood with a racially and socioeconically mixed population" with a focus on historical preservation, and just like now, residents were concerned about gentrification. Due to the city's focus on affordable housing, this did not happen, but the neighborhood stayed segregated. In 1992, OTR was criticized by the advocacy group Housing Opportunities Made Equal, saying that the neighborhood was a "permanent low-income, one-race ghetto—a stagnant, decaying 'reservation' for the poor at the doorstep of downtown." The demographics remained roughly the same until race riots erupted in 2001. To keep OTR poor and black might preserve some people's city, but it will be sparse and racially segregated, with high crime, low employment, and instability.

Gentrification can just be a derogatory word for social and economic integration. The goal of most housing policy is to create economically and racially diverse neighborhoods, yet there are few places where this diversity actually exists. With its 300 vacant buildings, OTR could be such a place. There is room for more middle-class white people without displacing current residents. In 2002, the city made plans for a balance of 50 percent market-rate housing with 50 percent affordable housing to be reached in the next five years, and that balance is still far away. Low-income residents could even benefit. As urban critic Lance Freeman said, "gentrification is often accompanied by new retail outlets, the refurbishing of housing and overall improvements in amenities and services." 3CDC also believes in this trickle-down effect, claiming the park will "stimulate additional private economic development, which will further improve the quality of life for the neighborhood and its residents." In OTR, improved amenities can be a larger park green and a splash ground, for instance, or a 50 percent drop in serious crime since 2001. Many homeless people I talked to were excited that the park would be more beautiful and roomier, though they were worried about being harassed.

So gentrification is not inherently bad; however, like the dog park, when it starts to replace things of value that are already in a neighborhood, you get into trouble. The pool is gone and so are the courts. Residents seemed resigned to the fact that a city can't change without losing something in the process. But what they ultimately want is mutual benefit. They want more homes and businesses for people like them. Their ultimate goal is more affordable housing built alongside the market-rate rehab. As Ricardo Taylor said, "Let us be a part of it too. Establish us as well. If you can't stop a locomotive, get on board. We accept that you renovate. But renovate us as well." The problem is that the state has stopped giving tax incentives to build affordable housing, and Section 8 reforms provide housing vouchers that allow stable low-income residents to live outside the city. Many affordable-housing developers have switched to market-rate development, which accelerates gentrification. While 3CDC does have a few units of affordable housing, housing advocates say there are not nearly enough units to meet demand. There's no counting system in place to make sure the neighborhood doesn't tip one way or the other.

I guess that's what I want. I don't want this neighborhood to tip. I want OTR to balance between "ghetto" and "dog park." How do you achieve that? How many percentages of the various income levels and racial demographics should we have? I don't know. I'm not an urban planner. But it seems that the obvious solution would be some formal mechanism of mutual benefit, such as using the tax revenue increases from market-rate development to build affordable housing, so that low-income residents have places to stay. All I know is that I want to have my OTR. I want to have spaces that are for me. I want to walk my dog to a state-of-the-art dog park and talk to people who bike to work and like the local Vietnamese restaurant, who enjoy good books and movies, and who bitch about drinks being too expensive at The Lackman on Vine Street. I want to celebrate this neighborhood's German history and admire its ancient buildings.

But I want others to have their OTR too. I want them to have their pools and basketball courts, their corner stores and barber shops, their community centers, schools and shelters. I want them to have their history too. And when I walk down the street, if I don't see Uncle James, if the homeless are gone, if my dog doesn't speak Spanish, if a black man doesn't call my dog "long and strong," and say it just like that, then I don't want to live here.

Not long after I wrote the first draft of this essay, I walked Betts to Northern Row while talking to my father on my cell phone. Inside stood a white hipster woman and a large, pit bull lab mix. I had never seen them before. Betts strained against the gate, but this time, I hesitated. "It's OK," the woman said. "He's friendly." I opened the gate and Betts sniffed the dog. After they both wagged their tails, I let her off the leash and they began to run around the courtyard. About a minute later, my father heard the phone drop, the woman screaming, "Oh my God! No! No! No!" and then the sound of sirens.

When the EMTs arrived, my right pointer finger wasn't where it was supposed to be. It's difficult to piece together what happened, but after the dog locked its jaw behind Betts' shoulder, after it shook and tore, after its jaws started to move lower and lower and I imagined Betts' entrails spilling out of her body, I lost it. I punched the dog's head, gouged its eye with my thumb, twisted its paws, and eventually found my hands near its jaws, trying to tear Betts' skin from its teeth. When they finally separated, I thought my dog was dead. Meanwhile, the top of my finger took a sharp right turn, just hanging there, torn open a few inches above the nail, my tendon poking out like a tiny gray feather. I didn't feel a thing.

After a dicey surgery and three days in the hospital, I was released a whole man. And somehow Betts was okay. She only had two deep puncture wounds in her side. When I got her home, her wound was stapled shut, but then became necrotic and opened back up. The vet told me I had to just "let it heal on its own." To prevent her from licking it, I dressed her in a T-shirt, but the wound leaked through the cloth, so she looked like she'd been shot. My hands were bandaged and my finger ached. Our safe space wasn't so safe anymore. I had stupidly trusted a complete stranger, let my dog play with a pit bull, and put my hands inside its jaws. And now we both looked ridiculous. I wanted to just hide in my apartment. But Betts was whining. She had to take a piss.

Originally published in the Fall/Winter 2012 issue of *Black Warrior Review.*

Price Hill Portraits

Michael Wilson

element

Pushing the Racial Dialogue in Cincinnati

Tifanci Ressl-Moyer

Tiffanei
Ressl-Moyer

Pushing the Racial Dialogue in Cincinnati

When I think about my experiences in Cincinnati in the context of the dark hue of my skin and kinkiness of my hair, a reel of uneasy experiences plays through my mind:

"You should have a better sense of humor," my boss told me once after making a joke about people that are black.

"I'm glad I'm not black, because I like my good hair," my roommate once informed me while she watches me struggle in the mirror with my locks.

"My brother has never dated a black girl, but he has dated trailer trash," a coworker laughs. She only gets uncomfortable and confused when I ask her about equating the two.

"You're a shoe-in. They need more black people to represent them on the other side of town."

"The University of Cincinnati doesn't graduate one out of three of their incoming freshman of African descent," a counselor urged black freshman to use tutors to even the alleged graduation gap.

"She calls black people nigger all the time, Tifanei. Like it's nothing! I don't know what to do," a friend (not from Cincinnati) told me about a native Cincinnatian who she roomed with.

"Tifanei, the general manager is racist, everyone knows it. There is no way he's going to let them hire you unless you want to be a 'busboy' or a bouncer," a friend whispers to me at the door of a popular establishment downtown. "He wouldn't even serve the UC football players until I promised him they were athletes."

"During the riots my friend was just walking downtown and black people beat him up; he was just minding his own business!" a friend tried to explain the stemming of racial tensions to me.

"Why would you date a white man? Are you tired of black men? Did someone do something to you?" a black colleague confronts me after I introduce him to my boyfriend at the time.

I can't say I'm native to Cincinnati. I lived there for four years and it's honestly the longest I have lived in any one city. While I lived there I never met anyone who denied Cincinnati's pride. Just the same, not a single person denied the segregationist structure that many prideful Cincinnati communities embody.

Even with the substantial African-American Cincinnati history, it's my humblest opinion that the segregated communities noticeably affect the consciousness of race-related issues and identity.

People will tell me that the racism I experienced was just ignorance and not in any way a representation of Cincinnati. But that's just not true. When you grow up in a community where integrating with people who don't look like you is not valued, then it affects how you identify and interact with others as an adult.

For a long time I felt that Cincinnati didn't want to be burdened by any anecdote of race. I started to realize, as I engaged more conversation, many people in Cincinnati don't feel like they have a safe place to discuss race among a diverse group of people.

As I started to learn more about black history in America, it became my nature to probe people around me for their opinions. I had probing conversations with a lot of Cincinnatians who identified as being white. They would tell me they never discuss race to address social problems or economic barriers, because it wasn't an obvious reality to them. It was a trend for people to tell me that they felt manipulated by the "race card."

I met a lot of people who identified as black, who only wanted to cross racial community lines when they needed a job or wanted to start a career. I witnessed many of same people, myself including, silently struggling with their identity, because they were trying to understand the difference between "success and failure" versus "suburbs and urban areas" versus "white and other." These are not easy conclusions to come to when homogeneous communities with clear socioeconomic distinctions are the accepted norm. Cincinnati is where I began to understand how the notion of beauty is affected by having so much pride in a homogenous community, especially when one community is considered more successful and educated than the other. I know I'm mostly a nomad at heart, but I fell in love with Cincinnati for many reasons – those reasons had nothing to do with race. The heartbreaking lack of racial-consciousness in Cincinnati will change, it has to, but it will take more than just hope. In my opinion it's going to need a shift in values towards heterogeneous community-building and a collective effort to address an individual responsibility that defies race. All hues of human color have to accept responsibility for the reality that we maintain by just "going about our business."

It's very, very hard to sum up a large and somewhat ambiguous topic, like being black. But, if I have to, I want to end by saying two things:

1) These are my very personal experiences. I am not Cincinnati, but my experiences are real. I don't blame people I met for anyone's struggle with beauty or success. I don't think that one neighborhood is right or wrong about their interpretation of race and what it really means for someone's livelihood. 2) I have lived in a lot of different cities around world. Cincinnati's segregation is unique in a lot of ways, but it's not unexpected in the framework of the United States. There are many cities that claim to be successful, but are disturbingly segregated at the expense of their youth and social growth. What is most important is that, in Cincinnati there are powerful minds and there is fiercely creative energy. These are imperative assets in the fight for structural change.

Originally published in a slightly modified form on *UrbanCincy.com* in February 2011.

The Freestore Foodbank

Curtis Sittenfeld

The Freestore Foodbank

Curtis Sittenfeld

In the early 1980s, when I was a student at Seven Hills School, an annual can drive culminated in a school-wide assembly just before Thanksgiving. We'd all be sitting on the bleachers in the gym, a bunch of older kids would haul out bags of canned tuna and tomato soup and peaches, several crowd-pleasing frozen turkeys would make an appearance, a teacher would announce the tally of how much we'd collectively amassed, and then we'd cheer—possibly for ourselves, but I like to think we were cheering for the larger notion of generosity.

Unlike more complicated, grown-up forms of philanthropy—black-tie balls, silent auctions, remainder annuity trusts—the logic of giving away, say, a jar of peanut butter was easy for a child, or at least for me, to understand: Some people have enough to eat, some people don't, and those of us who have enough ought to share our bounty with those who are hungry. Founded in 1971, the Freestore Foodbank has grown and expanded considerably since I was a child, but its core mission—to help people in Greater Cincinnati in the most basic, daily ways—remains. It now distributes 11 million pounds of food to hundreds of soup kitchens, day care centers, and homes for the elderly. It also helps individuals and families receive urgent medical care, find housing, and obtain jobs.

One Freestore Foodbank program caught my attention a couple of years ago: Cincinnati COOKS! Through it, unemployed adults train for jobs in the food service industry. And while they're learning to cook, they practice by fixing meals served in homeless shelters and at kids' after-school programs. Personally, I think Cincinnati COOKS! sounds so great—so practical and smart and creative—that I've made donations for its organizers to buy a new vacuum cleaner and a baker's table. I still don't have a very clear understanding of what a remainder annuity trust is, but it makes sense to me that if people are learning to bake, they better have a table.

I no longer live in Cincinnati, but I'll always be a Cincinnatian, and the Freestore Foodbank makes me proud of my hometown. It's a place that you hope you'll never need but are awfully glad it's there.

Originally published in the October 2007 issue of *Cincinnati Magazine.*

FOMO

Kate Westrich

Kate
Westrich

FOMO

From the ages of 16 to 21, I worked seasonally at King's Island, a local amusement park. The job was junk. I wore an ill-fitting polyester uniform, worked 12-hour shifts in all sorts of weather and executed pretty much the least skilled of unskilled labor. Most rides I worked, I would load people on, press a button until the ride stopped and then escort people out of the ride area. Then repeat that activity, ad nauseam.

Still, I have only fondness for my time at the amusement park. I experienced there a little micro-culture with distinct class hierarchy and cliques: rides, water park, characters, stores, games, food service. The type of work you did and the area in which you worked dictated your place in the (amusement park) world and I was firmly planted in the world of rides, turning a blind eye to what I viewed as the subpar classes around me.

As seems to prove true of any workplace, sometimes it's the people you work with who make the job worthwhile. No matter where I worked in the park, the social aspect was what made it fun. When people traffic was slow in Hanna-Barbera Land, we would play pranks on each other and yell jokes back and forth between rides. During late hours in Rivertown working on the Miami Valley Railroad, we would sing along to the country music blaring over the loudspeakers and dance up and down the train station, much to the amusement of the train engineers who sat nearby watching. If co-manning a ride during peak hours, we would invent games to play to help pass the time—long games of trivia, who could check safety bars the fastest, and who get away with saying the most outlandish thing without a guest noticing. Long hours of mindless work in a place filled with 16- to 20-year-olds, the network of dating occurring within the park was indescribable.

While putting in 60-hour work weeks, my time off should have been a treasure. Instead I experienced serious Fear Of Missing Out—FOMO. While at home I would wonder what new relationships were being formed and who was breaking up. I would miss getting to eat lunch with best friends or hanging out late in the evening with new crushes. While not at work, I wanted to be at work.

When I cut my ties to the amusement park, I did so thoroughly. I haven't been back in more than 10 years. My FOMO at the park ended as I got engrossed in the rest of life. Friends, college, other jobs, marriage. I also started being really interested in what was happening in Cincinnati.

I live close to downtown Cincinnati, work downtown, and find myself spending nearly all of my social time in the city. That started slowly. I grew up in suburban Loveland hearing that downtown wasn't safe and that there was nothing to do, messages I thoroughly bought into. But circumstances change, and cities change. As more bars started popping up, more good bands started being booked in local venues, and more veggie-friendly restaurants were opened, downtown became more and more attractive to me.

A while back, a funny thing happened, one which several people around me noticed. During one weekend, we had multiple awesome things to choose from for Friday night… for Saturday… for Saturday night… for Sunday.

The Saturday of that weekend, I walked in the Hudepohl 14k Brewery

Run with my husband, Jason, and one of my best friends, Frank. In salute to Cincinnati's Skyline Chili, we walked in the 3-way category, dressed as cats in support of the animal clinic where we all volunteer and tethered together for the duration of the race, per category rules. Walking with us, and running by us, were other groups in costumes, some dressed in tribute to the local game of cornhole, others as characters from *Toy Story*, still others as basketball players and more. All along the route, which was dotted with signs detailing Cincinnati's long history as a beer producer, residents stood outside their houses and cheered us on. Afterwards, we were greeted by friends who came to enjoy the post-race party with us. Sitting at picnic benches drinking pre-lunch beer—it was a brewery run, after all—we discussed our packed weekend.

The night before, Jason and I had opted to go to MidPoint Music Festival and listen to The Head and the Heart in historic Washington Park, where we ran into friends from different neighborhoods around Cincinnati. Then we went to the Contemporary Arts Center where we were blown away by a performance by Kishi Bashi. While all of this was happening, Frank and another friend were attending the nation's largest Oktoberfest in downtown Cincinnati. Sitting at the picnic bench, a friend told us about a man she met the night before, a British tourist in town for Oktoberfest, and I got my first inkling of that feeling from my old summer job. I was confident in my weekend choices, but had I missed out on some fun—on something better?

After the brewery run, I was attending a baby shower, then Jason and I were headed to a Battle of the Bands in Northern Kentucky, followed by a dinner of pizza in the Clifton Gaslight District. We were planning on a quiet Sunday at the Hyde Park Farmer's Market and getting ready for the coming week. Our friends all had different plans for the weekend. Suddenly here in this micro-culture of our city was a long list of things to choose from.

Oktoberfest was continuing through Sunday, with British tourists in attendance. The Cincinnati Reds played the Pittsburgh Pirates all three days that weekend and the Cincinnati Bengals battled the Cleveland Browns on Sunday. The Broadway musical *Ghost* was playing at the Aronoff Center for the Arts. At the Cincinnati Zombie Walk, people in full zombie attire would be walking to benefit the Freestore Foodbank. In Washington Park where we had enjoyed music, friends would shop from local crafters at the City Flea.

Cincinnati—the city where I used to believe there was nothing to do—was bustling!

And in truth, there was no choosing incorrectly. People participated in the world's largest chicken dance with George Takei and partied in lederhosen throughout Oktoberfest. The Reds and Bengals both lost their games, but fans were still able to cheer on their teams while enjoying the sun. I heard only positive feedback from people who saw *Ghost*. The Freestore Foodbank raised money for and awareness of their services. The MidPoint Music Festival had bands playing to smiling fans across the city and at the City Flea, local crafters connected with shoppers for their wares.

I can look back on that weekend and know I had fun and that my friends did as well, but can't help but wonder if I could have had more fun.

FOMO.

It's a good thing. Even if I might have made the wrong selection, I have never been more proud of my hometown as when I could describe FOMO to people… and they were experiencing it, too.

'08

#5things

Sam LeCure

Illustrations by Russell Ihrig

I.
Fresh Findlay produce

2.
Mt. Adams overlooks

3. 'And this one belongs to the Reds'

28
STONES
LANES

4.
Stone Bowling alley

5.
The square

Pete Rose

Jack Heffron

Pete Rose

Jack Heffron

You were the Cincinnati hero, the King Arthur of our local mythology. You embodied our fondest dreams of ourselves. We were with you as you barreled toward home in the 1970 All-Star game and when you broke Ty Cobb's hit record. We tasted the dust whenever you slid head first into a base. Johnny, Joe, and the Big Dog may have powered the Big Red Machine, but you drove it. And more than those others, you are ours. You are us.

True, you've always been rough around the edges. But who wants a choirboy at the plate in the World Series? We could look beyond your goofy hairstyles and your lack of erudition, because you were, most of all, a winner. You did far better with less talent than most of your opponents. That's the Cincinnati way. To the rest of the country we're nothing special. But what we lack in size and speed and pedigree we make up for in hard work and determination. Just like you.

But then you forgot you were a living metaphor for your hometown. You broke the Golden Rule of the game. And we saw that beneath the crown we gave you was just a guy on the make, always looking for the next deal—Charlie Hustle turned Charlie the Hustler. We sensed that all of the hits and runs and belly-flop slides and the racing to first after a walk were really about the dough, about the adrenaline rush, about you. When we heard the news we were shocked. When you continued to deny your actions year after year we were embarrassed for you and for ourselves. We knew you were both guilty and lying about it, and that's not the way we wanted the story to end. You were the fallen hero, a national disgrace. Some of us lived with you in denial. We believed you deserved the Hall of Fame. Compared to the pill-popping, dog-fighting, gun-carrying jocks today, your betting on ball games seems harmless. But all of that, we must admit, is beside the point. The game has one rule: Don't bet on the game. For some perverse, self-destructive reason, you had to break that rule.

And yet, we're going to admit it right now: We forgive you. We show our forgiveness whenever you come to town. We buy tickets, line up for your autograph, take your picture, give you standing ovations, and hang on your every word to the media. We visit your exhibit at our own Hall of Fame—to hell with those snobs in Cooperstown.

We forgive you, and that's saying a lot because we're not, as you know, a particularly forgiving kind of place. We tend to take a hard line on, well, everything. But we forgive you because we need you. When you were a winner, we were too. Nobody before or since made us feel quite so good about ourselves. You did it your way, and that's our way—nothing fancy, just grit and drive and sacrifice and teamwork, and the will to succeed. Those are the values we hold sacred, and for many years we relished seeing those values showcase on the national stage with "Cincinnati" written across your chest. We forgive because we can't forget. You are ours. You are us.

Originally published in the October 2007 issue of *Cincinnati Magazine*.

Great American Ballpark

John Curley

SEE YOUR LOCAL FORD DEALER
27

This Triste Little Town

Rebecca Morgan Frank

Rebecca
Morgan
Frank

This Triste Little Town

> Chicago sounds rough to the maker of verse.
> One comfort we have – Cincinnati sounds worse.
> – *Oliver Wendell Holmes*

It would be a cheap shot if I began this essay revealing that Jerry Springer was once the mayor of Cincinnati. I should begin by telling you that Cincinnati is also the birthplace of three presidents, as well as legends Pete Rose, Steven Spielberg, Neil Armstrong, and Doris Day. But I don't follow baseball or Hollywood blockbusters old or new, and it has been made clear to us that our space days are behind us. My desire to write about this peculiar city is not even original: writers have been grappling with Cincinnati since its heyday in the early nineteenth century, when pigs roamed the streets and the city bore the nickname Porkopolis. Henry Wadsworth Longfellow dubbed it the "Queen of the West" in his poem "Catawba Wine," which celebrates the city's vineyards:

And this Song of the Vine,
This greeting of mine,
The winds and the birds shall deliver,
To the Queen of the West,
In her garlands dressed,
On the banks of the Beautiful River.

Mark Twain, on the other hand, is rumored to have said something to the effect of "When the end of the world comes, I want to be in Cincinnati—it is always twenty years behind the times."

In the British television comedy *Book Club*, the heroine, a rather abrasive and naive Midwesterner who tries to make her way among the Brits by forming a book club, introduces herself to her collection of strangers: "I'm Claire, and I'm from Cincinnati, Ohio, the Buckeye state, which is actually a pretty big city in America even if you've never heard of it."

Claire didn't have to cross the pond to feel the need to defend her hometown. Americans themselves have usually at least heard of a show called *WKRP in Cincinnati* or have changed planes in the Cincinnati airport, a hub for a major airline. They don't always realize that the airport actually resides in Kentucky. But beyond these cultural references, Cincinnati is a city people seem to feel strongly about, whether it is the natives defending it or outsiders lambasting it. The results of a Pew Research Center study of where Americans want to live listed Cincinnati as one of the most undesirable places: out of a list of thirty cities, only Cleveland and Detroit ranked lower.

But I knew none of this when I headed westward to the city for a PhD program in literature and creative writing, inadvertently joining the lineage of the Disgruntled Outsider in this Midwestern city, a city that is not quite south and not quite east, not quite small and not quite large. After years of being exploited as an adjunct at two small colleges, living with roommates, and suffering various heartbreaks, Cincinnati seemed like an affordable oasis that would lead me to a more sustainable future.

In the two years that I lived there, the "Queen City" was crowned America's unhappiest city, ranked one of the top ten most segregated cities, and dubbed home of the most dangerous city neighborhood, while simultaneously winning a spot as one of the ten most livable cities according to *Outside* magazine. *Outside* said that Cincinnati was the city where one was most likely to see someone sporting lederhosen unironically. Known for its goetta and beer gardens, Cincinnati takes its German heritage seriously.

Frances Trollope wrote unhappily of her time there, and despite her diagnosis that "[t]hey have a theatre, which is, in fact, the only public amusement in this triste little town; but they seem to care very little about it, and either from economy or distaste, it is very poorly attended," this no longer holds true: Cincinnati now ranks number one in its number of community theaters, and many are well attended, as seem to be all of the arts events. I once attended an art exhibit in a hallway in an old loft building. The artist had stapled a Styrofoam peanut to the wall. The hallway was packed, and the refreshments of fresh dates and expensive cheeses were devoured by the constant flood of art lovers. First Fridays in the Over-the-Rhine neighborhood sends couples wandering between boarded storefronts and freshly painted galleries. An artist can find workspace and exhibit space for next to nothing.

Cincinnati is not a town void of industry or art. It traded in its history as Porkopolis, the pork capital of the nation, to later become home of Procter & Gamble, and the city supports a symphony and ballet company. The University has a highly rated design and architecture school, and its music conservatory is said to generate some of Broadway's young talents. The Cincinnati Art Museum, which is always free to the public, holds a history of a city that had both money and a taste for art, and the Taft Museum is no second to this with its holdings of European old master and nineteenth-century American paintings. Life in the 'Nati, as the natives sometimes refer to it, puts a premium on cultural improvements.

Cincinnati's reach towards culture dates back over 150 years, to the mid-nineteenth century, when Ralph Waldo Emerson came to do a series of lectures. In 1938, Louise Hastings, in her essay "Emerson in Cincinnati" in *The New England Quarterly*, reflected back on the Cincinnati of the time:

> *During Emerson's visit militia paraded through the almost impassably muddy streets, great droves of turkeys passed through the downtown section, and the pork season activities had made Deer Creek, the "butchering ground," literally red with blood. On the other hand, in 1851 Agassiz and a delegation from Cambridge had come out to attend the meeting of the American Association for the Advancement of Science. In the same year an attempt was made to establish a National Portrait Gallery by the purchase of Peale's Museum, a collection of notable portraits of distinguished early Americans. An interest in music that had grown through fifty years was just at the mid-century quickening. Portraits of Beethoven, Schubert, and Mozart hung in the beer gardens across the canal.*

Modern-day Cincinnati benefits greatly from those early investments in the arts. It was the ballet company that was my first introduction to Cincinnati. When I was a young teenager, an older friend I studied ballet with went to apprentice in the company, achieving what we had worked so hard toward during our childhoods. When her fellow students painted a racial slur on her locker, she left and returned to the diverse Mid-Atlantic city she had moved from. This was the last I'd heard of the city until the graduate creative writing program came on my radar.

Cincinnati is not a small town. Its population is over 333,000 spread over 78 square miles of hilly terrain. It's a city of rises, of generous trees, of views—if you are in the right part of town. The views from the City View tavern in Mt. Adams and from the heights of many of its abundant and expansive city parks, such as Eden Park and Mt. Lookout, are nothing short of lovely. Cincinnati's park system is remarkable in its expanse and upkeep.

But you look out on the most polluted river in the nation and breathe in some of the worst air quality. Cincinnati is a city of contradictions.

Cincinnati is known for the four-day race riot that happened in 2001. Afterwards, many restaurants and bars closed and moved across the river to Kentucky. Suburban patrons felt more comfortable, it seemed, crossing the river rather than facing their own downtown and what its crumbling and boarded buildings held: the city's racial issues and the problems of poverty and employment that black residents faced. In 2009, 25.7 percent of her residents were living in poverty: for black residents, the number rose to 34.3 percent.

The city is segregated. One set of data sets the population at 173,582 whites and 140,402 blacks, but the Clifton neighborhood near the university is primarily white, as are the affluent suburbs. In contrast, the decaying (or slightly gentrified, whichever label you'd like to reward it with) Over-the-Rhine neighborhood downtown is filled with African Americans, and white graduate students at the university often warn newcomers not to move there.

Natives of Cincinnati liked to point out the diversity of the gentrified neighborhood Northside, but an evening in the local taverns there reveals scores of urban/suburban hipsters, all white. The old stores and check cashing establishments seem to have different clientele: those who had been living in a damaged neighborhood for years, now parallel to those who came in and swept up houses and created a market for a cupcake bakery, tattoo parlors and salons, some upscale restaurants, and bars that offered vegan hotdogs and evenings like "Drunkass Bingo" attended by (white) guys in skinny jeans. Cincinnati's alternative culture plays out in its thriving record store and music scene, where you might find a band playing in what seems to be an abandoned brewery or in the Comet, which has punk, bluegrass, plenty of tattoos, and jerk tofu burritos. Cincinnati is a decent place to be a vegetarian.

The high African-American population is linked to the city's history as a place for African Americans to cross the Ohio into freedom. Of course, the Fugitive Slave Act of 1850 allowed slave owners to cross over and retrieve their "property"—the famous story of Margaret Granger, the woman who killed her children rather than let them be returned to slavery, is the source of Toni Morrison's famous novel *Beloved.*

Journalist Lafcadio Hearn, more known for his writings on New Orleans and Japan, spent almost a decade in Cincinnati writing for T*he Cincinnati Enquirer*, bringing to life sordid murders and seedy neighborhoods and life by the docks. In 1875, he was fired from *The Enquirer* for marrying an African American. A few years later, he left for New Orleans. He was eager to leave "beastly Cincinnati," where he felt "ostracized, tabooed, outlawed." He had indeed broken the law: interracial marriages were considered a crime.

The African-American population was mobilized in the 2008 presidential election of Barack Obama, swinging the conservative county to a democratic candidate for the first time in years. I walked from door to door, struck by the warmth of the people I met. I had lived in dozen of cities, and this was the first one where my canvassing would matter for a national election. I felt strangely empowered. Many of the organizers managing volunteers had come from out of state.

It's not rare for outsiders to comment on the internalized self-loathing and pride the natives sometimes show. At the first party I went to, I met a few locals.

I just moved here from Boston, I said.

Why, they said. And this was not a curious why, but an accusing one.

Or, as the notoriously snarky A.A. Gill of *Vanity Fair* said, in response to an online uproar by residents in reaction to his mention of Cincinnati in an article about the Creation Museum in nearby Kentucky, "There were, though, other things that I didn't mention that I did like about Cincinnati. There was the funny taxi driver who said, 'What the fuck did you come to Cincinnati for?'"

There is a website for outsiders, Cincinnati Imports, which has as its tagline, "Are you tired of people asking you what high school you went to?" This refers to the strange phenomenon of people referring to high school when they ask where you went to school (and this was amongst people with college and graduate degrees). Guest blogger Jane Friedman, former publisher of *Writers Digest* wrote, "My biggest goal when I moved to Cincinnati was to leave it as quickly as possible. That was in 1998. I was so miserable living in Cincinnati that each time I drove into town—always on 71/75 North or 74 West—I cried at the sight of "Cincinnati" on the green signs. Whenever I traveled to other cities or states, I'd apologize for being from Cincinnati, or say I was a rural Indiana girl." I myself wept each time the plane landed, when the taxi led me toward the Cincinnati skyline. There was something about the moment the plane struck earth that made me feel that everything had been lost. Of course, it was purely symbolic melodrama. We were landing in Kentucky.

Coming from the east coast, I felt at times like I had struck foreign land. I was the same person who had lived with different families in Atlanta and Pittsburgh as a child dancer, who'd left the South for boarding school in New England and college in New York, who had struck out for the West on my nineteenth summer to work at a dude ranch in Montana, where the cowboys in their tight Wrangler jeans and cowboy boots and hats had taught me to two-step and I'd learned to bake from scratch. I was the same person who had driven to the west coast, sight unseen, directly after college graduation, who'd once taken a last-minute job teaching children on 1400 acres in the Northwoods of Minnesota, who'd lived in the foothills of the Sierra Nevadas. I'd fallen for the depressed and sprawling city of Albuquerque, the overpriced and gorgeous hills of Boulder, the quirky small-town life of Marblehead, Massachusetts. I had always seen myself as fairly adaptable, had found friends within weeks in all of these places. But suddenly I was somewhere where strangers seemed taken aback if you spoke to them, a place where I was examined with a wary eye. Was it me or them? I was an Outsider, and it seemed there was nothing I could do about it.

An architect I met told me it had taken him twenty years to find his niche in the city. A friendly couple in their sixties that I met in a bar, at the only party I attended that was not University related, told me how they'd met a young woman who had worked at Procter & Gamble for two years, and how they were shocked that in the two years that she had been there, no one had invited her to their house for dinner. I didn't tell them that I knew how she felt. Sometimes it seemed as if by stating my previous residence I had uncouthly laid claim to royal heritage. But as a native of a small Southern town myself, I was confused. Any of the people I met could have moved to Boston or any other place as I had. I had moved all over the country, and while none of those places I'd been had become my permanent home, I had loved each of them in some way. Cincinnati residents seemed to be so monogamous in their city love, and to show affection for some other place was resented, as if loving another place was to disregard their home.

I had never met a place so difficult as Cincinnati. It never seemed to understand how much I wanted it to love me, how I had dreamt of this graduate program, this city, the mysterious future it would surely open for me.

My students were mostly from the Cincinnati area, although some were from other parts of Ohio, and the best class I taught was one on Ohio poets. My students understood the local. They soaked up Nikki Giovanni, Rita Dove, and Paul Laurence Dunbar, and they recognized familiar landscapes and towns in the poems of James Wright and in Alison Stine's first book. They warmed to Kevin Prufer's critique of America and Empire: he was one of their own. This was their world, their Ohio, and for the first time they spoke to me. The single mothers working and going to school, the twenty-something high school student teacher who still writes and asks me for suggestions for diverse poems to bring to the inner city schools where he now teaches full-time, the quiet and polite girls from small Ohio towns. They lived in a different Cincinnati than the graduate students, than the suburban hipsters with tattoos. Together, we read about rural Ohio, tried to understand its history, the beauty in the sometimes bleakness.

I regret that I didn't find more of a way into their Ohio beyond through these poets and what my students and I shared in them. Perhaps it was easier for me to want to understand the blood running through the streets and the rusting small towns and decaying urban buildings than the band-aid of white culture—highbrow or hipster—that part of the population tried to cover it up with. This was the Queen City. The City of Seven Hills, Cincy, Paris of America, the 'Nati, the place of which Frances Trollope said, "All animal wants are supplied profusely at Cincinnati, and at a very easy rate; but, alas! These go but a little way in the history of a day's enjoyment. The total and universal want of manners, both in males and females, is so remarkable, that I was constantly endeavoring to account for it. It certainly does not proceed from want of intellect."

You're beginning, I imagine, to question both of our judgments. But lest you think her cry is solely a judgment of Americans, or mine of Midwesterners, I should add that many I met from neighboring cities found the city problematic as well. "It's a difficult place," a woman from Louisville who had gone to school there told me.

No one seemed to love the place but the natives, and it seemed to take a good twenty years to become one.

What was it? There were cafes and bars, a few notable used bookstores, and I would go to them alone. A French boy who had moved to Ohio as a teen was charmingly kind to me at one of my favorite cafes. He told me about the plants he grew, and said, yes, this is a difficult place. You just have to change your mindset, he said.

But to what, exactly? I believed that it was me, that I was like a pebble in a wound of a city, and that I had to be dug out.

The New York Times reported on a Q&A following a reading at the 92nd Street Y, at which Lorrie Moore and Jonathan Franzen were asked why Midwesterners were funny, funnier than New Yorkers. Moore said, "All the funny ones get on a bus," while Franzen said, "The people who leave the Midwest, leave it behind, have probably developed some coping skills, such as flight. And people who can master one coping skill may be able to master another one, such as humor." But the *Times* articles ends with Moore's veiled nip at Cincinnati, where she had recently given a reading: "After thinking about it, though," she added: "The place that's not so funny is central Pennsylvania and southern Ohio."

Around me, my fellow students bought real estate, one declaring bankruptcy at the end of school, another failing classes as he was sinking all of his time and money into repairing the house. The graduate students' wives began to have babies. I joined the private library, marveled at the beautiful woodwork. A journalist friend of a friend of mine became my solace.

Where are we? we asked. In the library we met a Canadian woman writing her dissertation. She told us how for the first weeks there she had wept as she watched the rows of garage doors in her cold neighborhood rise and fall like clockwork for the workday, leaving her standing with her son in the driveway.

Mommy, why are you crying? he asked.

We'd tell this story and laugh; we'd collect evidence of our shared despair as outsiders that didn't want in. We shared discoveries which ranged from puzzling to horrific: covers over *Cosmopolitan* in the grocery store checkout line; the fact that Cincinnati was the birthplace of Charles Manson; pickaninny dolls found at a neighbor's yard sale.

One day I opened my inbox to find that the department chair had sent us a quote from a former faculty member and writer, Dallas Wiebe, found in Nelson W. Aldrich's book on George Plimpton, *George Being George*:

> *I was stuck out here in this provincial town called Cincinnati. It's really a backward swamp down here, certainly in a literary sense. It was kind of a de profundis thing, you know, calling out from the depths. It was wonderful to be in* The Paris Review, *because that was away from this place. When* Skyblue the Badass *came out from Paris Review Editions, the dean of the College of Arts and Sciences wanted to fire me. I didn't know anything about it until it was over. There was a group in the city called the Citizens for Decent Literature; that group proliferated. It was in other cities, too. They became Citizens for Decency and then they became Citizens for Community Values. They're still here. They're the kind of people that if they don't like what you do, they'll try to punish you. It's not just a matter of criticizing you or of dealing with you—they go after people. It's happened a lot here in Cincinnati. It's not just me.*

(Later in the excerpt, he goes on to reveal that the leader in the charge to fire him was none other than Charles Keating.)

Was the chair, like Dallas, myself, Frances Trollope, Mark Twain, and so many others, experiencing this *de profundis*? Or was he commenting on how much he believed things had changed? Perhaps the most mysterious thing about Cincinnati was that I believe it was both. That the ardent defense held a loathing, like an internalized self that the city and its inhabitants couldn't seem to shake. To push out outsiders was to push away the chance to be judged. It was the oldest junior high trick in the book, and yet I continued to fall for it.

Emerson made several trips more to Cincinnati for lectures. His first visit had met with cries of "Pantheist," and a resistance that melted away over the years as he gained a following. But when he spoke up for John Brown, *The Enquirer*, the local newspaper, ran the following: "[his] appearance upon the stand will be a public scandal... The utterance of this blasphemous and traiterous sentiment; this applauding of robbery and murder, of rapine and insurrection; this insult to everything which men hold sacred, ought to debar its author from the recognition of any community which has a proper declaration of opinion which involves moral guilt and turpitude of a high character... "

Maybe some of us just didn't belong in this city.

One day I was walking down the giant hill from the university, weeping in the rain. I had never felt this alone, not when living in a cabin on twenty acres, not when away from home in boarding school for months as a small girl.

A woman stopped me. She was a scientist from India. She took me in her arms and hugged me. We were fellow international students it seemed—strangers in a strange land.

"This is a difficult place," she said.

This was a refrain I heard from people who'd lived there thirty years, people who had once lived there, people who lived in the nearby cities of Columbus and Louisville. How could a city be difficult, like it was a person with a capricious or unyielding personality? How was one to make peace in such a relationship?

I wanted to understand this personified city, to unwrap this city as a metaphor. But it remained an enigma, and it remained an adversary.

On leaving, Trollope said, "We left nought to regret at Cincinnati. The only regret was, that we had ever entered it; for we had wasted health, time, and money there." Lafcadio Hearn wrote to a friend that, "It is time for a fellow to get out of Cincinnati when they begin to call it the Paris of America."

How could the natives believe they lived in an oasis, a place of perpetual renaissance and culture, when their guests felt something so radically different? Was it the natives who kept the outsiders at bay, or the outsiders who simply couldn't see what was before them?

In springtime in Cincinnati, the magnolias reign, and soon the fireflies introduce their mating dance, evoking a magical world of nature within the city. When I left, my married friends bought a house and made a garden, a music room, and a writing room—a life I couldn't dare to dream of back in Boston. Another friend started a bilingual reading series and continued to run a poetry series that grew in a generous space of an old school turned artist building. The editors that I knew continued to make incredible handmade magazines and one opened an art space that hosts events. Real estate was open, offering space for community and creation. The bars had ample outdoor seating, and the city was once again in bloom.

This strange habitat would not hold some of us, and we bit back. Perhaps our loathing, too, held its opposite. A longing for the history, space, ease and continuity that our lives could not hold. And a bitterness toward those who were so sure they had found something that they were willing to block the rest of the world out. Maybe to all of us, Cincinnati is the end of what stays the same. And one part of the equation frightens each of us.

Growing Up Half-Black in Cincinnati

Alex Schutte

Alex
Schutte

Growing Up Half-Black in Cincinnati

Cincinnati's history has long been shaped by the ethnic makeup and cultures of its inhabitants. Some of the biggest contributors to Cincinnati's history and culture have been African Americans and German Americans. I embody this history, quite literally, as I am half-black and half-white. My African American mother, oldest of ten, grew up in the projects of Cincinnati, while my father grew up in a German Catholic family in Finneytown.

Navigating the world as a biracial child can be tricky. While I grew up within a very loving family, sometimes it was difficult to figure out where I fit in to the traditional American racial dichotomy. I could never be white but I was never black enough. Most white people assumed I was 100 percent black until they saw my father. American society has always followed a "one drop" rule for classifying individuals as black if they had any ounce of African ancestry. On the other hand, many black people thought I must be mixed with something because I had that "good hair." I eventually began to self-identify as black, although I never denied my father's blood.

Over the years I became more and more proud to be black, seeking out more information about black history and the story of blacks in America. It turned out that I was living in a city that has been highly influential in shaping the history of African Americans – a city whose history is intertwined with the lives of many African Americans who have struggled for equality and freedom.

YOUTH AND SCHOOL

In grade school we learned of Cincinnati's role as a border town between a free state and a slave state. Our river town played a key role in the Underground Railroad, serving as headquarters to abolitionists, white and black, helping slaves escape across the Ohio River to freedom. I learned the names of important historical Cincinnatians such as Harriet Beecher Stowe, Levi Coffin, and John Rankin. Years later, the National Underground Railroad Freedom Center would be built along the banks of the Ohio River to recognize and celebrate Cincinnati's vital role during this period of time.

Growing up within the Cincinnati Public School district allowed me to meet and befriend others from all walks of life. At a young age I began to see a pattern in the neighborhoods kids said they were from. Kids that were from Hyde Park, Anderson and Madiera were white and had money. Kids that were from Bond Hill, Avondale and Walnut Hills were black and had no money. I grew up in Kennedy Heights, so I was really middle-of-the-road. There was a sizeable black population, but I didn't live in the hood either. I felt like I could tell my black friends I lived in Kennedy Heights (aka "K-Heights!") and get their approval, but still be able to tell my white friends where I lived without them being scared to come over.

When it came time to choosing a high school, there was only one clear choice—Walnut Hills High School. This was by far the best traditional high school (I'm excluding School for Creative & Performing Arts on this one) at the time within the Cincinnati Public School District. I was either going there or my parents would pay to put me into Seven Hills or a similar school. Fortunately I passed the entrance exam and was accepted into Walnut; however several of my grade school friends did not pass. Instead of Walnut, my black friends went to Taft, Woodward, or Withrow. While my white friends' parents paid to get them into private schools.

Even the mighty Walnut Hills was not safe from racial tension though. Looking out into the lunch room you still saw segregated social groups. Once I got into honors classes I became separated from several of my black friends from grade school. I observed shades of what I refer to as segregation, although I never saw any explicit racial conflicts or anything close to the law-mandated school segregation of decades earlier.

A HISTORY OF TENSION

I'm a mid 80's baby, so I didn't get to experience Over-the-Rhine's Main Street in its heyday. However I can vividly remember my cousins on both sides telling tales of going out and having a blast on Main Street. Main Street used to be THE place to go out, no matter if you were white or black. There was a spot for everyone. And then there was the summer of 2001.

Timothy Thomas, an unarmed 19-year-old black man was shot and killed by a white police officer. At the time, Cincinnati had a largely white police force and had already experienced several clashes between police and the blacks in the community that year. The Timothy Thomas shooting was the proverbial straw that broke the black community's back.

Over-the-Rhine and the center of Cincinnati erupted in riots, and a city-wide curfew was issued by then Mayor Charlie Luken. I was in high school when all of this was going on and I can remember how crazy I thought it was for an entire city to be under curfew. I mean my parents always had a curfew for me during the week, but now even they had a curfew! This was not Cincinnati's first race riot. The first was in 1829 when anti-abolitionists attacked blacks in the city. Riots occurred again in 1836, 1841 and later in 1968 after the assassination of Dr. Martin Luther King Jr. After the 2001 riot the city was in need of healing and dialogue.

A SOBER HOPE FOR THE FUTURE

Our city is still recovering from the wounds of 2001 with some suburbanites afraid to go all the way downtown. We are a city that never forgets and is slow to move on. We love clinging to the past whether that past is good or bad

However, Cincinnati has come a long way since then despite all this. A new generation of Cincinnatians has embraced our city and its once forgotten central heart. This new generation has forgiven the city of its past and is willing to put the rest of this town on its back, dragging us toward our true potential. While I embrace the new development in our city center, and within its historic neighborhoods, I am sometimes torn as often times these new developments require the removal of lower income (mostly black) people.

In the second half of the twentieth century, predominately white working-class families who had filled the urban core during the European immigration boom in the nineteenth century moved out to the suburbs. Blacks filled these older city neighborhoods. Putting myself in the shoes of these inner city inhabitants I'd say "Where the hell have you guys been? You moved out, I moved in, and now because you decide to all of a sudden care about this neighborhood again, you're kicking me out and telling me I'm not good enough to live here?"

I hope the new generation of Cincinnatians will care about not only our city's rich historical, cultural and architectural treasures, but also care about the people who have helped shape them and who have called them home over the years. Cincinnati can become the city that we want it to be but only if we all work together to improve the lives of everyone who calls our city home.

Originally published on *UrbanCincy.com* in February 2011.

Personal Botany

Garrett Cummins

Garrett Cummins

Personal Botany

Like my maternal grandparents who lived in different parts of Cincinnati, at different times in their lives, I have lived, worked, or dated someone from just about every part of Cincinnati. I've been stoned, sober, paranoid, married, divorced, broke, well-off, and a good and bad student here as well. But what does that have to do with Cincinnati? How has Cincinnati cultivated and allowed me to bloom through the years?

I call myself a Cincinnati native, but that's an understatement. Though my last name isn't common here, it is part of the name of a small neighborhood called "Cumminsville." As far as I know, neither the paternal nor maternal sides of my family ever lived there. However, there is a street in Cumminsville named "Lillie." This odd intersection of Cummins/Lillie did unknowingly forecast the Cummins/Lillie biological gene swap that is yours truly.

According to my mother, the Lillie family (of German descent) lived in Wooden Shoe Hollow, now called Winton Woods. Back in the mid-1800's, German families lived there and raised flower gardens. Though wooden shoes are primarily associated with the Dutch, the Germans actually wear them a lot—especially when gardening. These Wooden Shoe gardeners sold their flowers (lilies, tulips, etc.) at the then-new Findlay Market in Over-the-Rhine. Grandpa Lillie's family, like the other German families, busked their blooms to other Cincinnatians. Even after Grandpa Lillie left Nanny and moved to Florida in 1973, until he passed away in October of 1992, he had flower gardens, teeming with panoply of color.

My maternal grandmother came up from Raleigh, North Carolina to Cincinnati on a boxcar, at the age of 14. She passed herself off as 18 to get a job at Crosley Radio. She occupied a coldwater flat with her sister Ruby and a co-worker. She was half Irish and half Native American; she grew flowers and vegetables of all sorts once she moved out to Cherry Grove in Clermont County. So, Nanny (nee Crough) Lillie drifted here, following the rails to Cincinnati.

As my maternal grandparents' marriage wilted, my mother and father also divorced. Around the time of their divorce, my mom and I relocated to Anderson Township. I was a country sprout from Bethel, Ohio, who didn't know anything about Procter & Gamble's bedroom suburbs, of which Anderson Township is one. Bethel didn't produce soccer moms, station wagons, 24-hour stores, and yuppies. As I saw it, everything and everyone erupted from the new blacktop and gray stone. P&G employed many of my classmates' fathers, and some of their mothers too. By contrast, I was a wild, curly-headed, bumpkin weed, not bred to bloom in some suburban garden. My new classmates and neighbors got planted in Anderson as young bulbs and bloom into some beautiful, upper middle daisy, lily, or rose, ready to be displayed in some bouquet of sports, marching band, and honor roll.

As I blossomed toward adulthood, I grew taller than the manicured lawns, shrubs, and eye-level rose bushes. With such height, Cincinnati shone on me and fed my dreams of a larger plot, a better land to thrive in. Unlike these suburban, hothouse flowers, I had Lillie running through me. I had just as much right, if not more, to flourish and grow in Cincinnati. I had to venture beyond the darkened, walled garden of the east-side suburbs. As a senior, the Queen City light shone on Clifton's colorful denizens, and backlit signs advertised gallery openings, street fairs.

My first attempt to root in Clifton didn't take. I rode the winds of my whim; drifting from Ohio University to Long Island, then back to Clifton. Sure, I blossomed once I transplanted to Five Towns College on Long Island, but my first marriage withered while still on the vine. Even when I came back to Cincinnati, I couldn't cultivate my second marriage. I lost sight of the light my young eyes once knew and followed. Now I know what these failures to flourish came from: I forgot how Clifton nourished me.

Years later, while living with a friend across the street from Deaconess Hospital and the University of Cincinnati, I spotted my greenhouse out my bedroom window. The University stood there, reflecting its light back into my past, not on my maternal grandparents, but on my mother. She, too, blossomed professionally at UC. Looking at that building, a part of Cincinnati's beacon, I said to myself, "I'm going work there," pointing at the buildings I could see.

Now, the house across from Deaconess is gone; the hospital made it a parking lot. But I'm still thriving. I've been a composition instructor at UC since 2012. Besides my love for UC's program, I also love a particular tree in Clifton. Every fall since I started going to UC in 2008, I wait for the first tree to turn color in McMicken Commons. When autumn comes, that single maple blushes and flames orange, with just a hint of rust. The orange vibrates in every picture I've taken. Such a strange juxtaposition of foliage and fire. The comparison works well; when I see that tree standing tall, I root down into my own passion.

Despite how much I've grown, both personally and professionally in

Clifton's nurturing grounds, I've found myself bending towards the light of Northside. All I have to do is walk over the Ludlow or Harrison Viaduct to places like WordPlay, where I am a volunteer writing tutor. My teaching and tutoring profession reminds me that I am an offshoot of my gardening ancestors. Instead of pruning and raising plants, flowers and vegetables, I teach and tutor writing to young (and not so young) people, helping them blossom, mentally and emotionally.

Unless some foreign beacon finds me, compelling me to uproot, I'm staying here, cultivating literacy with my students, while blooming as a postsecondary writing educator. I've gone from being just a blossom to a reflection of how Cincinnati radiates.

First City/ Polyphonic Monuments

Cedric Michael Cox

Conversations with Irma

Katie Laur

Katie
Lau

Conversations with Irma

On hot, muggy Cincinnati summer days, I get in my car and head for Irma Lazarus' swimming pool. I drive my old Ford up the elegantly curved blacktop lane to the Lazarus house, past the patch of watercress that Irma planted many years ago in a cool stream of water that trickles from the top of the hill. When I park and walk through the gate, into the shade of the massive oak tree, the temperature seems to drop ten degrees. Suddenly, the Springer spaniels are upon me, jumping and whimpering with excitement, their whole bodies wagging along with their tails. The male, Sean, has a green tennis ball in his mouth and his big brown eyes are shining and hopeful, but I am firm and walk down the stairs to the terrace.

Irma lies stretched out in her Brown Jordan chaise longue under a modern-styled canopy, the famous Lazarus Lizards darting across the hot bricks into rocky crevices. Over the tops of the trees behind her, I can see the river and the skyscrapers of downtown Cincinnati, the city which Irma Lazarus helped to shape as surely as any politician or public figure in the history of the city.

"Hello, darling," she says, looking up from the book she is reading which is wrapped in a yellow Mercantile Library dust cover, and gives me a smile. I take her hand and give it a light squeeze.

"How are you today," I ask, for she has been ill a while now.

"Not good," she replies, in a matter of fact way, and changes the subject.

"You know," she says, "I love looking at my trees now. They're like the marks you put on the door to measure yourself when you're a child; I can tell my age from them."

She points to a large tree of pale green, almost yellow, standing with the others that line the drive.

"That's a rain tree," she says. "I don't think there's really a Raintree County in Indiana, but years ago, when that movie came out, I planted the tree as a sapling. Now look how big it has grown. It's almost luminous, don't you think?"

She is right. Once I notice it, my eyes return to it again and again.

The north end of the Hyde Park grounds surrounding her house are thick with wild flowers and a few dogwood and redbud trees that bloom sweetly in the spring. Everything is quiet here, like a nature preserve. Before she was ill, Irma was an avid gardener, and on the summer days when I came to swim, she'd be pulling weeds like a driven woman. I might find an entire theater company in the pool or as I did one day, Mikhail Baryshnikov poised on the diving board in a leopard-skin bikini, the tiny ballerinas in his troupe sitting in lounge chairs on the terrace, stitching their pink satin toe shoes like fairies.

"I bought this land for $3,000 while Fred was in France in World War II," she says, waving her hand over her domain, "and everybody told me I was crazy. Fred's brother told me I would not like my neighbors. Everyone else said it was simply not the 'in' neighborhood. I bought it anyway," she says, pausing to take a swat at Sybil who is pawing at her legs.

"I'm impressed with how much better disciplined these dogs are since Ashley Stephenson's first visit," I say, my tongue in my cheek.

Irma laughs happily at the mention of his name. "Wasn't he simply wonderful," Irma says.

Ashley Stephenson was the Queen's Royal Horticulturist, and he came from London a few years ago to judge the Cincinnati Flower and Garden Show. Sean and Sybil had been pups then and completely out of control. On the last Sunday of his visit, the weekend of the Kentucky Derby, Fred made mint juleps so potent that after drinking just one, the Queen's Royal Horticulturist stopped talking about the Latin names for plants and loosened up enough to share with us his favorite recipe for spotted dick.

"Let me show you how I discipline the Queen's dogs," he said. He stood; Sean and Sybil jumped on him, and he took the two fingers of his right hand and brought them down sharply on their noses. The dogs sat down instantly and looked surprised; discipline was an altogether new concept for them. "You see," Stephenson said, "you just give them a thwack."

We were all on our second mint juleps by then, and Irma and I were so amused by the word "thwack" that later whenever one of us said it, both of us would giggle uncontrollably. A few days later the whole affair was just a dim memory to Sean and Sybil, and they were worse than ever.

"Once I bought the land," Irma says, talking about her house, "I had an aerial photograph taken and sent to Fred—he was stationed in France—and he was enthusiastic about it. He consulted a number of European artisans, and we began to plan the house. My sister Eleanor's husband, Carl Strauss, designed it."

She looks happily at her house, a weathered modern-looking Bauhaus kind of structure, sitting at the end of the driveway. It is unpretentious, with a glassed-in room on the lowest level and a long patio on the second level, connected by a stone stairway lined with tall old cactus plants.

"Did you notice the clematis this spring?" she asks, and I nod enthusiastically. It curled around the trellis by the driveway, its blossoms vivid purple.

She sits up, away from the back support of the lounge, takes off her straw hat and pulls her white hair into a pin high on her head. At 81, she still wears the dramatic dark glasses, the Irma Lazarus eyelashes. Nobody in Cincinnati can pull off glamour as well as she.

First of all, it's the company she keeps: her friends are captains of industry, prominent politicians and the cream of the arts world. Then, for all her public persona, she has always been a private, occasionally inaccessible person for whom the telephone is anathema. Another component of her glamour is her daring sense of fashion. When someone complimented her on her outfit at a gala one night, she said she had her dressmaker whip it up out of the late conductor Thomas Schippers' white eyelet curtains. According to Fred, she once had an evening coat made from a brightly colored shawl she bought at a Goodwill store, and she wore it to a symphony function in New York City. In the Times the next day, there was a picture of three society women: Mrs. So-and-So in her Oscar de la Renta, Mrs. Such-and-Such in her Givenchy, and Mrs. Fred Lazarus III whose outfit came from Goodwill.

She wore miniskirts and black fishnet stockings in the 70s and boogalooed at discos until the wee hours of the morning; then the next day she'd be up and on the road by 6:30 a.m., stumping for the Ohio Arts Council—which she and Fred nurtured through its infancy—or driving somewhere giving speeches to promote the Orchestra. During this time (when she was also raising five children), she hosted her own television show on the arts on WCET, called *Conversations with Irma*, on the air for more than thirty-five years. Once a week, she interviewed notables such as her dear friends, Leonard Bernstein, Beverly Sills, Aaron Copland, Carol Channing and Roberta Peters. She has said that her most fascinating interview was with the composer Wagner's grandson, who talked about skinheads and anti-Semitism. Of the Copland interview, "I wish Channel 48 hadn't destroyed it—or reused it, whatever they did—because it was his seventy-fifth birthday, and he said something surprising to me. He said that as he aged, ideas still bubbled up inside him as much as they ever had, but that he felt less urgent about them. I'd have expected just the opposite."

Irma raises herself from her chair and walks slowly towards the pool. "It's time for my exercises," she says cheerfully. "A therapist came to the house and prescribed them to strengthen my arms and legs." She wades into the cold water and begins to lift one leg slowly and painfully against the weight of the water.

She talks while she does her movements. "I knew twelve conductors well in my lifetime; they stayed at my house from time to time. One Thanksgiving, Eric Linsdorf and his wife cooked Thanksgiving dinner for Fred and me and Michael Gielen and Bernie Rubenstein. Having three of them at the same time was a bit risky naturally—we could all hear Linsdorf ordering his wife about in the kitchen—but it turned out fine, and we had a great dinner.

"Of course, my favorite was Lenny," she says, smiling, speaking of Leonard Bernstein, whose career she guided and nurtured. "Lenny always used to say that praising an artist was like pouring sugar through a sieve; they can't get enough of it."

"How wonderful it must have been to know him," I say, and she nods her head.

"He threw himself into everything, all his energy, all his passion he brought to everything he did. But he could get carried away with himself sometimes, and his wife, Felicia, was quite good for him. She'd prick his balloons," Irma laughs and begins to stretch her arms. "There is a famous story about a conductor who died while waving his baton about, and Lenny got quite emotional and said he simply couldn't think of a better way to go. Felicia thought about it a while and said, 'I think I'd rather go at Bloomingdale's.'

"I met Lenny here in Cincinnati when he came to audition for a job which he didn't get, and then later Fred and I were at Aspen, and Lenny was staying there as well, trying to be incognito, which was ridiculous. Absolutely everybody knew it was him. I wrote him a note saying that Fred and I were staying at the same hotel and asking him to ring us. He did and he said, 'Irma, you have to teach me to ski.' I said I had never taught anybody, but his instructor kept following him around, wanting to talk about his own interpretation of Brahms, so I agreed to do it. I went to the gift shop and bought a very small replica of the Norse snow god for him. As we climbed higher on the lift, I thought what if he can't even get down the slope, but I needn't have worried. He was a wild reckless skier, and when he started down the slope, people just scattered in every direction, getting out of his way. He was absolutely fearless."

The spaniels are tugging relentlessly at Irma's arm. When she finally throws the tennis ball into the swimming pool, the dogs run as fast as they can, each of them trying to reach the ball first. It is Sybil who plunges into the pool and climbs out with it grasped tightly in her jaws. Sean is waiting, and with a growl and a bit of bullying, takes the ball away from her and trots proudly with it back to his mistress. Irma shakes her head. "She does all the work," she said, "and he gets all the glory. It's still a man's world.

"I was working at the Symphony with a man I admired a lot, and he came to me one day and said, 'Irma, you really ought to be Chairman of the Board of the Symphony, but of course that's impossible. You're a woman. The Chairman of the Board has to be a man.' I told him he was right of course. When I was a young volunteer, I was quite outspoken. I didn't like the conductor, and there were a number of other things I felt were needed to make this a first-class orchestra. One day I got a call from the president of the Symphony, asking for an appointment to meet with me, and I thought, 'Uh-oh, I'm going to get told to keep my mouth shut.' Instead, he wanted to ask me to head up the Women's Committee, because, as he put it, 'we've never had a Jewish woman do that.'"

Irma pulls herself cautiously out of the pool, smiling at the ironies of a world she has already begun to shut out.

"But why did you do it all?" I blurt. "And where did you get the energy?" It is something I have always wanted to ask.

"Well, darling," she says slowly, "I was born privileged, and to tell the truth, I have always felt a little guilty about it. My twin sister, Eleanor, and I were born after my parents had been married seven years. They wanted children badly, and all of a sudden they got twin girls. We had a German fraulein, which was the thing in those days, and my father would walk behind her when she was strolling us down the avenue so that he could overhear the oohs and ahhs and 'aren't they precious' comments from the other people as they passed us on the sidewalk. He was so proud of us.

"Then, too," she says, lowering herself carefully into her chair on the terrace, "my mother was a classical singer. She gave recitals and sang professionally, really, and of course they went regularly to the opera, so I grew up loving music. When I was at Smith College, the emphasis was on involvement, working to make the world a better place, that sort of thing. But in the end," she says, finally stretched out again on the lounge chair, "volunteering is simply a way of life in Cincinnati, more than any other place I've ever been."

We are both quiet for awhile, and I see she has nodded off for her afternoon nap. I slide quietly into the cool water and begin my laps, but my mind is crowded with memories of Irma and Fred, the color and excitement they have always brought to everyday events. I remember swimming here late one night after performing in 100-degree heat at a bluegrass festival at Stone Valley. I was tired and grumpy at the festival, and suddenly Irma and Fred and a group of Spanish expatriates they had befriended, pulled onto the festival grounds in Fred's black Mercedes. Irma has always been at her best in unbearable heat, and she had brought a picnic basket with her. I had told her that most folks did this at bluegrass festivals so they can sit in the shade listening to the music as long as they wanted. But I was dismayed at the contents of her basket. Instead of fried chicken or ham sandwiches, she had brought pate and wafer-thin water biscuits, a plate of sliced tomatoes dressed in oil and fresh basil leaves, a chocolate bundt cake, and of course a couple of excellent white wines from Fred's cellar instead of a six-pack of Pabst Blue Ribbon. I laughed and told her she hadn't got it quite right, but all of us sat under a shade tree and ate happily, and my cross mood dissolved instantly.

I stop swimming at the end of the pool and shake the wet hair out of my eyes. When I look up, a shaft of sunlight is illuminating Irma's raintree. It is a moment of pure enchantment, and suddenly my mind calls up my loveliest memory of Irma and Fred.

It all happened on an otherwise dull night at Arnold's, downtown, where I used to sing on Tuesday nights with a swingy jazz band called the Rhythm Rangers. Fred and Irma came in one night with a group of friends after a Playhouse performance. Irma was dressed in Thomas Schippers' curtains that night, as I remember, and she looked as beautiful as I had ever seen her, her salt and pepper hair freshly coiffed, her smile radiant.

She danced for a while with Morrie Jacobs, her favorite partner in those days, and they looked to me like something out of a movie. I sang "Mean to Me" for her, and as the room became more crowded, she and Morrie danced themselves out the back door and onto the sidewalk. The band was playing "Rose Room," and Irma and Morrie were whirling around the sidewalk like Fred Astaire and Ginger Rogers. I watched them through the window, and presently Fred went outside and tapped Morrie on the shoulder and cut in. I walked quietly out the door to watch them. The moon was nearly full, and the fruit trees in front of Arnold's were just beginning to blossom. Fred gathered Irma into his arms quite naturally and said to her in a sort of sexy way, "Irma, I don't think you're allowed to dance on the sidewalks."

They danced together cheek-to-cheek, down the sidewalk, away from me, but I could see them as they passed beneath the streetlights, and the notes of the clarinetist, playing "Rose Room," wafted sweetly on the night air.

Originally published in the September 1993 issue of *Cincinnati Magazine.*

Queen City Grooves

David Bottoms

David
Bottoms

Queen City Grooves

All metaphysics and causality jazz aside, how often does it transpire that a spur-of-the-moment decision results in the undertaking of a task that feels like personal destiny?

Not often, I'm guessing, which is why I was so dumbstruck when I realized it was happening to me.

In October 1992 I moved—largely of caprice and with no job, contacts, or plan—to Cincinnati. The chamber of commerce had sent me a brochure, it looked like a nice place, so the decision was made.

Upon my arrival I was stunned by a sense of familiarity…of recognition. The place seemed like something that suited me, and I it. The neighborhoods, the hills, the high narrow houses set on short, deep lots seemed so alive, so vibrant and distinctive. I loved it from that first evening, when I finished unpacking and left the U-Haul on Volkert while I repaired to Lenhardt's for a beer and some schnitzel.

Being back in a larger city awakened an old interest, that of record collecting. Only two years before, in a mall near Chicago, I'd gotten a nasty shock—a record store with no records! On vinyl, that is. The place was filled with CDs and that quaint vestigial format, the cassette. How nice, then, to browse among racks and racks of cool stuff at places like Yahoo!, Mr. Happy's, Wizard's, Mole's, Ozarka, Circle, Parker's and Everybody's.

There was also (amid the endless record-stacked warrens of the Northside junk-joints) a place called Dave's Emporium. I stepped in one day and met the proprietor. Great place! Did he have any records? Sure. Up from the basement came box after box of 45s, which I, being of humble wallet, looked through with a combination of amazement, lust, and internal admonitions toward restraint. "Hey," he noted, "all those that say 'King' and 'Federal' and 'Fraternity'? Those are from here."

I was floored. My adopted city had a recording past. But why was there no greater knowledge of these labels among the public at large? I then received a delicate bit of insight about my new town. Words to the effect of, well, the place having a "conservative" streak. Of its reluctance, especially in olden times, to make much hay about raucous pop music. Subsequent inquiries put to other folks confirmed this phenomenon.

As I'd begun classes at UC, I asked around the *News Record* if they needed any entertainment writers. So began some great times in the newsroom as I watched my reviews go from galleys to newsprint for all to read. A story idea grew as well: a capsule history of this local record-label activity I'd been studying. The piece, "Stacks of Wax: Fifty Years of Cincinnati Record Labels" appeared in the March 3, 1994 issue of *Panorama*, the paper's weekly arts & entertainment supplement.

As spring edged closer I felt a little flash of inspiration/madness. I'd write a book about the city's musical and recording history. No one else had done so. Why shouldn't it fall to me? My wife at the time, Laura, expressed trepidation (and rightfully so, as we had a child on the way), but still supported the idea. As a history and culture freak and a record collector with a new calling, I was doubly damned. So began an odyssey of digging, querying, and searches for music—all in the years before the internet—and a great many drafts.

Cincinnati in 1994 followed the exploits of Bill Clinton, Marge Schott, and Bill Cunningham, and once every few years a piece would appear in the papers about the recordings and stars of the past. Such pieces were dutifully titled along the lines of "When King was King," and so forth, and while they did discuss the marquee names from those years (James Brown, Hank Ballard and the Midnighters, Bonnie Lou, The Delmore Brothers and even local performers such as Katie Laur) there was the sense that there was more there. That turned out to be precisely the case.

An acquaintance steered me toward a 94 year-old bluesman named James "Pigmeat" Jarrett, who'd been coaxed out of retirement in '79 and performed from time to time. He paused after one evening set, pivoted to straddle the piano bench, and fished a filterless Pall Mall from its pack. I cursed the ambient crowd noise as he spoke of the past, with a small, knowing smile and the hard-won wisdom of the years. Interviewing him one humid summer evening, he spoke of the Newport of the '20s: of being sent for in a big car and swept away to lavish parties where huge amounts of food, liquor and money repaid a busy night's playing. "If you got it here," he said, pointing to his head, "and here," pointing to his heart, "you gonna have it here," whereupon the raising of his ancient and wondrous hands said all that needed to be said about his life and music.

His assistant, Carolyn, directed me to one Philip Paul, then working for the Council on Aging. Paul and his wife Juanita spent several gracious hours discussing the frantic life of a drummer who'd left New York to play with Tiny Bradshaw's hot R&B outfit—touring with them always included packed dates at Cincinnati's Cotton Club at Sixth and Mound—as well as becoming a house drummer for King Records. Paul experienced the thrill and tension of King's endless production as the label met the demand for both their R&B and "hillbilly" offerings, to say nothing of catching the energy of the post-rock 'n' roll furor for vocal-group numbers, or remastering sessions to add a different beat or strings or such to address trends like Mambo or Bossa Nova...

Housemate Dave Miller got me on as a DJ for WVXU's Nightwaves, which, in addition to being a great opportunity in its own right, introduced me to guys like engineer George Zahn. Zahn had a master tape of Jon Hartley Fox's "King of the Queen City" radio production, which discussed the rise of Syd Nathan and the audacious birth and subsequent flourishing of his label. Furthermore, WVXU was at the time remastering Ruth Lyons' Christmas albums, harkening back to the magical era when Lyons, and such programs as her 50-50 Club, drew the city together like no one before or since.

Dave lived in Cheviot (which I dutifully learned to pronounce as "Chivviot"), and only a few moments from his house sat Counterpart Studios, home and psychic base of Norman Howard Lovdal, who had since the '50s been known as DJ, producer, engineer, author, publicist and historian Shad O'Shea. O'Shea was enthralled by the biz, fascinated as he first spun those black-plastic bombshells then went on to produce them himself. He learned firsthand the industry's highs and especially lows, as a hot track he'd produced ("Hey Conductor" by the Mark V) got shut down cold by emergent power-pollster Bill Gavin because of a veiled pot reference. In '75 he took over the reins of Harry Carlson's Fraternity label, begun in 1954 and run out of the Sheraton-Gibson hotel downtown almost to the end. Carlson had spent his life in Nebraska, Illinois, and Ohio, and split hastily for Florida.

Fraternity producer Carl Edmondson loved Carlson (as did literally everyone who knew and worked with him), but also remembered that his business acumen sometimes took a back seat to his enthusiasm for a song or his love and appreciation of an artist. Faced with a smash such as "Memphis" or "Wham!" by Lonnie Mack or "Then You Can Tell Me Goodbye" by the Casinos, Harry dug deeply into his own pocket to cover parties, promotions, trips, and so forth so that everyone could share in his discovery. Writer/historian Randy McNutt laughs and remembers Carlson responding to queries about a song's chances (or anything at all, really) with "Fabulous. Faaabulous. They're screaming for it in the streets."

We don't see that kind of man anymore.

Kentucky boy Rusty York recalled moving to Cincinnati in the early '50s and playing what he and his bandmates knew only as "fast country," as there was no other name for it. After cutting a Marty Robbins track called "Sugaree" for a tiny local label he had it picked up by the mighty Chess label of Chicago, and before he knew it was at the Hollywood Bowl as part of the inaugural rock'n' roll show at that now-storied coliseum. Driving down the street one day in Cincinnati he heard the song issuing from a car radio, then from another car as well, on another station! He began the Jewel label on Kinney Avenue in Mt. Healthy in 1961, and began to deliver years of gospel, pop, and down-home rural sounds.

With regard to radio, Dusty Rhodes was a young boss-jock in upstate New York who was well-acquainted with King Records' acts: he took two copies of Bill Doggett's "Honky Tonk" and then, using two turntables, seamlessly segued from part one to part two. He relocated to the Queen City and became one of the "Good Guys" on 1360 AM, the powerhouse WSAI, and was instrumental in bringing the Beatles to Cincinnati in 1964.

He remembers those years as bracing, every day a surprise, as you never knew what differing sounds would and could jostle and nudge for a chance at that endless sea of teen radios.

I traveled out to the West Side to meet Scott Cheesebrew, caretaker of his dad's vast holdings in vintage vinyl, for a further deepening of my knowledge of local label doings, and there also lucked into an interview with Chuck Seitz, who'd served as Chief Engineer at King from the late '50s though 1963. Seitz took over a studio setup that was completely utilitarian, a "hand-built affair," that scarcely kept out the din of production from the floor. Day in and day out he manned the recording process, and was there for the introduction of stereo into the production arsenal. One associate, Dave Harrison, developed a console that became known as the "Harrison Board" throughout the industry.

Each person, it seemed, led to another, and my hands were full. I filled spiral-bound notebooks with notes, ideas, outline refinements, interview transcriptions, phone numbers, and other relevant scribblings. The depth of the manuscript increased, the breadth, and with it, the scope. Meeting a fellow named Frank Powers gave me an afternoon's worth of insight into the city's musical milieu in the '20s, when every hotel of any significance had its own band, and every tavern and gin joint for a hundred-mile radius boomed with music, laughter, and life. He supplied me with a two-cassette compilation of these long-forgotten acts, and another piece of the city's story fell into place. From minstrelsy to ragtime to jazz and burlesque, the tale and its pursuit gripped me completely.

Accordingly, meeting Mike Smith was a coup. Smith was a kid who hung around King in the '60s and saw much. As a resident of Evanston he had pride of ownership in the label's hot streak of the time. Sometimes acting as gofer, he was privy to much of the day-to-day atmosphere at 1540

Brewster Place, from hirings and firings to artists who—owing to not having had a hit for a while— ended up painting or mowing grass out behind the studio. Syd Nathan made time for kids like Mike, once gleefully confiding in a group of them: "Yes, I admit it. I'm funky. I'm funky Mr. Nathan," then, leaning in conspiratorially, "...and I got soul." Mike spoke of a man who clambered into an aged station wagon and drove through the neighborhoods, handing out newly pressed 45s with a bag of Husman's chips stapled to the paper sleeve, shouting "Get 'cho King Records here!" all the while.

It was also convenient for a James Brown or Marva Whitney to have such kids around, kids who could be dispatched to White Castle for a sack of burgers, or a "red Dana," the local soda favored by Brown.

Smith's recollections weren't all flattering, and several of his recollections weren't for publication, owing to legal troubles or even physical danger to either one or both of us. His memories brought to life for me the lot of black Cincinnatians in the '50s and '60s, of segregated shopping days in the city's stores, of the thrill of seeing black faces in a Doublemint commercial, of the dark days of 1967-68, when entire swaths of the city were shut down, roadblocked, locked down and under the muzzles of machine guns and even tanks. "You'll want to talk with Charles Spurling," he told me after several interview sessions, as he could see I was serious and wanted the entire story, blemishes and all.

Spurling lived in Lincoln Heights, and had been a recording artist, writer and producer at King. He used to stick up for the Isley Brothers when they were just kids bopping around town, and he wrote the song "Shout!" for them, a song based on the energy of his youth in the Sanctified church. He had that song deftly spirited away with no thanks (along with the Miracles' "Mickey's Monkey," but that's another story), and had a rough time at King as well. Smith claimed that it was Spurling who wrote "Papa's Got a Brand New Bag," and lost that song as well as subsequent efforts amid the supernova of the peak Brown years.

These "soul" years were further expounded upon by a cat named Kenny Smith, who before plying the insurance trade with State Farm was a fixture in the bustling local clubs. The manuscript's continuum kept growing, with that live excitement that stretched from the Cotton Club and Castle Farm to WCPO's *Myles Foland's TV Dance Party* and the sockhops from Withrow High School to Coney Island's rocking dance floor.

A post-divorce acceptance into a doctoral program sent my ex to Houston, and though I bid Cincinnati a morose farewell I was able, through the now-exploding internet, to continue research, contacts and interviews for the book, as well as keep my desire alive to return to the city, to help nurture and shepherd its efforts to preserve, celebrate and keep its musical history living and vibrant.

The first volume of this history is ready for press, and it's nothing less than the debt I owe the Queen City: my friends there, my life there.

Scott
Devendorf

Called Home

Over the Rhine

Just shy of Breakin' Down
There's a bend in the road that I have found
Called home
Take a left at loneliness
There's a place to find forgiveness
Called home
With clouds adrift across the sky
Like heaven's laundry hung to dry
You slowly feel it all will be revealed
Where evening shadows come to fall
On the awful and the beautiful
Every wound you feel that needs to heal
And silence yearns to hear herself
Some long lost memory rings a bell
Called home
Old pre-Civil War brick house
Standin' tall and straight somehow
Called home
Mailbox full of weariness
And a word of hard won happiness
Called home
Leave behind your Sunday best
You know we couldn't care a less
Out here we've learned to leave the edges wild
And stories they get passed around
And laughter – it gets handed down
Read it in the lines around a smile
Our bodies' motion comes to rest
When we are at last
Called home

"Called Home" appears on the 2012 album *Meet Me At The Edge Of The World.*

Neither Created Nor Destroyed

Jenny Ustick

Jenny
Ustick

Neither Created Nor Destroyed

Heat. We generate it when we are well-nourished and when we move and work, hold onto it when well-insulated, and we feel it in response to passion, pressure, and change. It's been on my mind lately because as I write this, Cincinnati is in the midst of one of a string of snow and ice events—actual polar vortices—that have come infrequently enough in recent memory to warrant a monopoly of news coverage for days before and after the first flake falls. At least it seems that events like these just don't occur as often or as intensely as they did when I was a kid. My first winter on earth was the last time the Ohio River froze at Cincinnati, and there hasn't been a winter as cold here since. I thought the reliably snowy winters of my childhood—those in which I learned to make angels and build men, and hurled myself downhill on a smooth disc as fast and as far as possible—were a thing of the past. In the late '80s, though, we returned to our "normal," and here we are.

I fancy myself a type of hipster homesteader, but I'm only in the beginning stages. I know the techniques and own the equipment, but I am at peace with modern conveniences and ingrained habits. My husband and I grow an impressive garden (now in its third year), but we don't yet go as far as keeping chickens. I love buying local food, but still enjoy my organic bananas and coffee. Out of penance and aspirational righteousness, we conserve more and consume less whenever and wherever we can. We compost, recycle just about everything, and generate very little actual trash. Almost all of our light bulbs are compact fluorescents or LEDs. And because of the recent cold snap and our insistence on a thermostat set at 62 degrees, some nights we build a fire—a real wood fire—in the fireplace. Not long ago, I tried assembling one of those tea light flowerpot heaters blowing up the Internet (and unfortunately some homes) at the moment, and decided that pulling on another layer of clothing was just as effective.

One reason energy consumption is a concern in my household is to offset the twenty-mile drive between my job teaching at the University of Cincinnati and our house in the eastern suburbs of Cincinnati. At most times of day or night, the trip can take between 15 and 20 minutes. During rush hour, however, I can count on doubling that.

On a recent drive home, as warmth from my car's engine was finally reaching my toes and I was putting distance between myself and the city, I realized that there is something similar about us commuters and the way the heat in my car works: convection. We move fluidly (and sometimes not so fluidly) in and out of the city limits, from neighborhood to neighborhood, through cuts in the rolling hills and in all the cardinal directions. It is a cycle, an exchange of capital, of information, and ideas. We leave our contributions, and we get things in return. And it's not just true of me and my job and my automobile, but the history of the city and the people who have built its character.

These days, many people assume (understandably) that I live closer to the urban core (and those who know me but have never visited my home have the idea that I live "way far out"). I am often seen "in town", have a lot of business there, and care a great deal about its goings on. Alas, I am an outsider. I know well what it means to exist in the physical and social margins while playing an active role in shaping this city's identity.

The young people who would become my great-grandparents came to Cincinnati around the early 1920s. They came from as near as Northern Kentucky, and as far as Nürnberg, Germany. The Germans, Georg and Kunigunde, opened a bakery on Liberty Street in Over-the-Rhine. They spent time at Grammer's restaurant, which hosted the German Singing Baker's society. But at that time, anti-German sentiment and the ravages of prohibition must have so disillusioned them that they eventually left the basin. They moved outward down the Mill Creek Valley and opened another bakery in Elmwood Place. Georg's uncle Albert, who had settled in Reading years before and sponsored Georg's immigration, was likely a draw in that direction. They did well there, becoming a fixture of the community, and raising a son, Herman, my grandfather, who learned the family trade. Herman would eventually begin working at Procter & Gamble's Ivorydale Plant and stay there until he retired.

Perched high up on a Mt. Auburn hillside, in a neighborhood called Little Bethlehem (nestled in the shadow of Christ Hospital), were the homes where a few generations of my mother's family lived. They hailed from places like Corbin, Irvine, and Ravenna, Kentucky. I like to romanticize their story as part of the Appalachian migration, imagining that they were one-tankers (as opposed to two-tankers, who could afford that second tank of gas to make it to Detroit, Cleveland, or Chicago). But the truth is, there was a conscious choice to settle here—and stay here. There was movement, an exchange of energy and human resources, back and forth between coal country, Dayton's industry, and Cincinnati. My relatives worked the Baltimore and Ohio Railroad, contributed to WPA projects, and owned or worked for small businesses repairing the city's diverse, aging architecture. Then in 1962, my mother's family had scraped together enough to build a small brick and frame house near the border of Mt. Washington in Anderson Township. Mt. Auburn, which had been described as a suburb a century earlier, was now part of a crowded city they found difficult to navigate with three children in their early teens in one small second-floor apartment. My grandparents had spent much of their own youth in houses within a small radius, in that same neighborhood on a steep hill. With hard work, they had managed to buy a little bit of space on a perfectly flat lot, not far from my Pappaw's father, Wilson. Eventually, there would be five children. They put in an above ground pool. They had hit the big time.

Going back generations, my family has been on the outside (of something) looking in, while somehow embodying a few places on a list of defining characteristics of Cincinnati. Whether it's being a German immigrant in America between two World Wars, coming to the big city from small town Appalachia, or moving from the inner city to a suburb where your style and personality don't always mesh with the prevailing attitude or behavior (picture me as a toddler being pulled by my Gran down Salem Avenue in a little red wagon and leaning up against a case of Bürger Beer), there has always been an awareness of our dissimilarity to our neighbors. I have to believe that a good many Cincinnatians—most of us coming from working class families—may know this feeling.

It isn't just about money. Neighborhoods in this city were established by people coming from villages tucked into hillsides (elsewhere in the United States and overseas), and their residents were often suspicious of outsiders. They were accustomed to turning inward and relying on their neighbors—

people of the same cultural type—for their social and practical needs. It's the reason why today, even with ever-changing demographics, Cincinnatians, when meeting someone, ask their new acquaintance where they attended high school. It serves as shorthand for a great deal of information, and cuts down on the volume of small talk. Even if the assumptions are completely wrong, in the mind of the person who asked, it answers these questions:

"What kind of person am I dealing with? What are her/his values? What is her/his socioeconomic class? What, if any, cultural touchstones do we share?"

While I'm certain the need to know one's alma mater still exists in some circles, in the ones I travel it has been pared down to a simple question of where one lays their head. What is your neighborhood?

A couple of years ago I was invited to a lovely courtyard gathering of a friend living in Over-the-Rhine. The friend is a transplant from another state, and I did not know any of the other guests at the party. I was making small talk with a man who sold real estate, and the conversation inevitably turned to my dwelling place. When I told him where I live (which for youngins, West-siders, transplants, and even lifelong city dwellers requires a geography lesson), I watched his face change from an inquisitive gaze to one of disdain. I tried to recount my own adventures in real estate with him, but he wasn't interested in hearing how it was I came to own a house out there. I was being openly judged because of my zip code.

The courtyard incident stands out to me because the exchange was almost comically stylized. Most often, when explaining where I live, the reaction is one of confusion—about geography and about me: in their minds, I don't fit the profile. Often there are questions about driving routes or whether I live in the country or not. But that's as far as it goes. This man clearly felt comfortable casting negative judgment as though I were incapable of relating to him about anything at all. He didn't know me, but began making assumptions as soon as he heard the word "suburb"—after which he heard nothing. He may have wondered, "what's this conservative stay-at-home soccer mom with 2.5 children doing at this party after dark in Over-the-Rhine? Doesn't she have oranges to slice?"

There I was, a guest in the courtyard of my new friend, literally in the inner circle of his home, and feeling again like an outsider. Just as the real estate agent proudly described bringing new residents to his neighborhood, I had hoped to talk about my work and connection to the city, about how I contribute despite my address. I would have loved to tell him the story of my family and how I am both woven into and wrapped in this odd, old tapestry of a town.

We do ourselves a disservice by tying assumptions about one's philosophy, allegiance, or usefulness to proximity. I don't have to live in the city proper, or want to, in order to do good work in the city. You don't have to live in the suburbs. You don't have to want to live in the suburbs. Neither of us should hold that against one another. In fact, you might be surprised at how much we have in common.

Just as natives often return to Cincinnati after having lived in another city, neighborhoods can have the same boomerang effect. After my mother's family made their move east, the area has remained our collective home base, even after spells in other places. First it was my parents moving back across Beechmont Levee to Anderson Township (near my grandparents) when I was a toddler, after living in Mt. Lookout. Then my brother and I made our own circles, living in places like the Brewery District (well before it was a hot spot), Oakley, Newport, and Covington before going back home. We returned at various times and different reasons. He now lives in our late grandparents' house on that flat corner lot.

In 2002, as newlyweds, my husband and I bought a house in Union

Township (an adjacent suburb to Anderson Township) near where Beechmont Avenue and Interstate 275 cross. After searching for properties in many neighborhoods we settled on our house because of its large yard, mature trees, and yes, an aboveground pool. We got a lot for the money. This was a year before I would complete my first project with ArtWorks and begin graduate school. I had no idea what changes those choices would bring. I was just proud to be a homeowner with plenty of friends and my folks nearby.

After getting my MFA I began working as an adjunct at a handful of universities, and had insane commutes. In the beginning, there were two days a week I had an 88-mile commute to Hamilton and back. Two other days, I taught at two locations and drove a grand total of 162 miles per day. Thankfully my situation improved.

In 2008 I accepted a visiting faculty position in Michigan, and we were faced with the decision of what to do with our house. Not wanting to sell because the economy was tanking, we decided to become landlords and rent it out while we were gone, knowing that we would likely return. In 2011 we did just that and have been here ever since.

We enjoyed our time in Michigan tremendously. I was given a wonderful professional opportunity, and we had a chance to get to know another place. Instead of renting an apartment in Heritage Hill or somewhere near the zoo in the heart of Grand Rapids, we opted for renting a house a half a mile from the beach in the town of Grand Haven on Lake Michigan.

It was no coincidence that, like our house in Cincinnati, the house was miles away from my job. Why? It comes down to priorities of ample green space, peace and quiet, a fenced-in yard, a slower pace of life, proximity to state parks, and the grandeur of living next to one of the Great Lakes. Aside from the large inland sea in our backyard, one major difference between here and there was that in Grand Haven we lived in a walkable community and took advantage of that. We would come to miss that quite a bit.

Despite our attempts to immerse ourselves in our new town, there were two developments tightening ties to my hometown while we were away. Just before moving north in 2008, I completed my first of six murals in Cincinnati with ArtWorks, on the Joseph House near the intersection of Vine and Liberty streets. It was called Over-the-Rhine: Into its Renaissance; this title proved to be accurate. The next two summers, we opted to leave the gorgeous singing sands of the beach behind to return to Cincinnati so I could work on two more murals in Clifton Heights and North Fairmount. In the nine months between mural projects, and until moving back, I kept close tabs on developments in Cincinnati, particularly in Over-the-Rhine. During our three years away, the Streetcar went from an idea to a plan, and was bolstered by the defeat of a referendum.

The second development, riding the social media wave and joining Facebook, allowed me to keep up with the chatter. I saw how people felt about what was happening in Cincinnati, and how this medium emboldened people to make public the opinions previously discussed in private company. It was ugly what people were saying. A vocal opposition had united in the form of groups like COAST (Coalition Opposed to Additional Spending and Taxes), and no wonder Streetcar supporters felt like they were at war. The Streetcar was polarizing subject, and I watched the debate unfold from 400 miles away.

So here we are again. It's been an eventful winter. It is during this time of year when commuting has the added challenge of snow-covered streets and highways, and makes me acutely aware of the drawbacks of being car-dependent. The Streetcar's future was once again uncertain. But, thanks to a new round of petitions prompting a vote on a charter amendment, it's moving forward. And like last time, I didn't sign the petition. Not because of my opinion on the project, but because I don't live in the city. I don't even live in Hamilton County, though I do have a Cincinnati mailing address.

I bought a house where I did because it pleased me. But there's a little bit of habit and inheritance in there, too. My father commuted from Anderson to Elmwood Place—his stomping ground—for decades before his company moved to Sharonville. My mother attended UC, and worked downtown at places like Pogue's and Baylis Brothers while living on the east side. It has never seemed outrageous.

While I don't consider my commute outrageous when compared to what someone in Liberty Township or Mason might face (or worse, what I used to drive in my early days as an adjunct), I'd like to drive less. I think often of moving closer to the city, but not into the center. Even if my husband and I were in a position to move (which we're not), it would be a tall order to find something that checks all the boxes. I do want to live in a walkable community, but I don't want to share walls with anyone. I want an unpolluted, sunny patch of dirt to grow food, and space for my dogs to run. Oh, and it would be nice to have a pool, and to find a deal that competes with our $407 mortgage payments.

We have no real connection with our neighbors in part because there are no sidewalks to connect us. We have no children but live in a community designed to nurture them. We belong to no religion. Our social center is elsewhere, and that's OK. I have a lot of friends who want to live, work, and socialize within a four-mile radius and do so, and I'm happy for them. But when I am home, I like to be home. I like having space between myself and the other functions of my life. Space to recharge my batteries.

I would be happy to share my story with the real estate agent I met in the courtyard. He wasn't necessarily being rude. He is just clearly energized by constant contact with others, and might not extensively consider the world outside his own. Plus, people moving downtown is good for his bottom line. I get it. In our conversation, I might learn that he wasn't born in Cincinnati, and isn't pulled in multiple directions by history, employment, and family; he might be content meeting all of his needs in one neighborhood. And he would learn that I move in different ways, and over different paths than he.

For me it is about energy. I make public art in the city, and I teach students at an urban university and apprentices from all over this region about pursuing art as a career. I value the core, and have from a young age thanks to parents who demonstrated its importance and made sure I was familiar with its bones. I am part of a dynamic, inclusive, expansive network of creative individuals who direct their energy toward the community and make it an attractive place to be. I have friends and acquaintances from places like Washington State, Oklahoma, Michigan, Connecticut, New Jersey, Montana, Colorado, North Carolina, New York, Nebraska, and Virginia who have chosen to make their homes here and have brought ideas and energy with them. They are invited to get involved on many levels, and they do.

Not surprisingly, I have noticed that people who are "from away" have some of the loudest voices on local issues—some more serious than others. Some complain in one breath about suburbanites who are disconnected from the city and reluctant to spend time downtown, then in the next breath, complain about the suburbanites who come downtown and get in the way of their urban utopia. Still, I appreciate some of the tremendously thoughtful pieces written by transplants about redevelopment and progress in the city, particularly regarding the Streetcar; these are people who are truly advancing the conversation. I'm glad they have chosen to call my city home. It is always refreshing to hear from someone who isn't mired in the inherited suspicion of neighborhood xenophobia because they weren't born and raised here.

That said, there is sometimes a bias against the suburbs that is likely just fear or lack of interest in the unknown ("you live where?"), and it conveniently fits with a progressive stance on urbanism. The sentiment is that this region and its growth are dependent on a vibrant urban core—to neglect progress in the core will have a negative impact on everyone. I agree wholeheartedly. But (and maybe it goes without saying), the core cannot survive without everyone. In other words, the core needs all 52 neighborhoods, the suburbs and (like it or not), even the entities that originally stimulated or grew along with the sprawl, too.

Small farms, distribution companies, manufacturers, educational institutions, social services, shipping, and construction are some of the things that exist in greater Cincinnati that make a comfortable, functional, and enjoyable life possible. We are intertwined by the production and consumption of goods and services, and by the ways in which we share and exchange them.

I completely understand why many transplants gravitate toward the basin. It is, after all, places like Over-the-Rhine that make attractive national news—now because of gourmet hot dogs and artisan cocktails, not race riots like in 2001. Anyone who decides to settle there should feel proud knowing that they are carrying on a tradition of the neighborhood being a landing spot for generations of people looking for opportunity. That story is true on both sides of my family. But my family benefitted from those opportunities, and decided to move outward into the growing region. That was the nature of things in their time. Nowadays, it seems that young people are as likely to relocate to another city as they are to retire here (or both, as many know, because it's hard to stay away from Cincinnati for too long). But more interestingly, we are seeing a movement of people from the suburbs back toward the center. Frequently, instead of people moving out of the city because they've improved their station in life, they're moving back. And some longtime city residents are being priced out of the market.

They are moving to the suburbs to save money, not necessarily because they want to leave the city behind.

I started venturing off on my own downtown shortly after *Little Man Tate* was filmed (not to suggest cause and effect, just timing). My friends and I would go to Kaldi's (now Park + Vine) and try and absorb the city by osmosis. Then it was going dancing at the Warehouse. Then it was working downtown, and now it's working on public art projects and other improvements—really working, if only in small ways, to invest my energy. I am drawn to the city and I always have been. But I always return to my little hidey-hole in the outer limits. From a short distance, and throughout childhood, I've watched the skyline change, businesses come and go and change names, and neighborhoods transform through demolition and gentrification.

I took personal interest in the story of a classmate of my mother's at Anderson High School, Buddy Gray, who was born in my neighborhood and was drawn to the city in a different way, moving to Over-the-Rhine and fighting for the rights of the homeless and disenfranchised. I awkwardly understand his fight against the district's addition to the National Register of Historic Places, but am admittedly giddy at seeing vacant nineteenth-century buildings breathe new life. Since beginning work on my first mural on Vine Street at Liberty, I have watched the neighborhood in the blocks to the south transform to an almost unrecognizable state. I wonder what Buddy would say about the neighborhood now, and about the Drop Inn Center partnering with 3CDC and preparing to move out of Over-the-Rhine.

But let's face it—it's easy for me to be wishy-washy on the gentrification issue because I'm not a resident of the neighborhood. I see both sides of the argument. The same is true of the Streetcar. I understand why some residents and organizations—many who are concerned with the Streetcar's impact on poor residents—oppose the project. I understand why some people would rather see resources distributed differently or in other neighborhoods. Yet, I support the project. Though it won't impact my daily life as far as I can foresee, I do see it as a positive step toward something I have wanted to see for a long time—light rail in Cincinnati. I do have a vote at the county and state levels, and will support rail components of the Eastern Corridor project. At a celebration of the December charter amendment victory where people were shedding tears of joy, I felt like a bit of an interloper. You see, I wasn't riding the same kind of buzz they were. I'm excited to see the Streetcar be built—really. But as infrastructure goes, I'd sooner benefit from the dreaded MLK Interchange on my commute to UC as a visiting assistant professor than from Phase I of the Streetcar itself. But bring it on, and let's see where it leads.

Not surprisingly, the extreme cold that has befallen us actually started freezing the Ohio River again. Also unsurprising was the on-schedule denial of climate change by people who don't understand that weather and climate are not the same thing. Despite many hopes and prayers (really?) and waxing poetic about '81 and '88, on the Sunday the polar vortex arrived the Bengals would again go one-and-done in the playoffs against the San Diego Chargers, despite a "sold out" crowd and fans who could suspend their disbelief long enough to think that their team could pull out a victory. Until they didn't, and talk inevitably turned to what a perennial letdown the Bengals are, and to how everyone knew exactly on whom or what to pin the blame.

For some people, politics are like sports. They've chosen a side, and they stick with it in good times and in bad, often exercising willful ignorance about anyone who thinks differently than they do. There is often no dialogue, no give-and-take. The other team is the enemy, and because we want something to happen badly enough (or because we want to be right), we believe it can happen.

I believe everyone agrees that growth for Cincinnati is what's wanted, but disagree about how that should look. It's undeniable that expansion is occurring. I believe we are at a critical point in how we shape ourselves going forward. Are we becoming a bigger city? If we are, we need to consider where everyone is coming from and where they are going—physically and philosophically.

While there are people who don't believe that humans are the cause of climate change, there are people who don't believe Cincinnati can, should, or will change either. There are casual doubters, and there are agents of stasis on one side; there are cheerleaders, and there are activists on the other. It's hard to deny that Cincinnati is changing, and (with the exception of those few extra degrees every August) I like what I see. I like that I can be a part of it, even from what some would consider afar, even from the outside.

If my husband and I are to stay here (that's the hope—that professionally Cincinnati can nurture us, and we will contribute in return) we would most likely move to one of the inner-ring suburbs—the first wave, maybe the one where I was born—for the sidewalks, the trees, and the shorter commute. Who knows—maybe there'll be a rail line there one day. That means I am thinking about my future in Cincinnati. And isn't that really the point? I'm looking forward to the work I have to do here, and there's a lot of it. Even if we go, don't worry—we'll be back, no doubt receiving a warm welcome and bringing plenty of ideas. That's how the transfer of energy works.

Cincinnatus

Aaron
Delamatre

LUCIUS Q. CINCINNATUS IN "LET'S GO BACK TO CINCINNATI"

BY AARON DELAMATRE

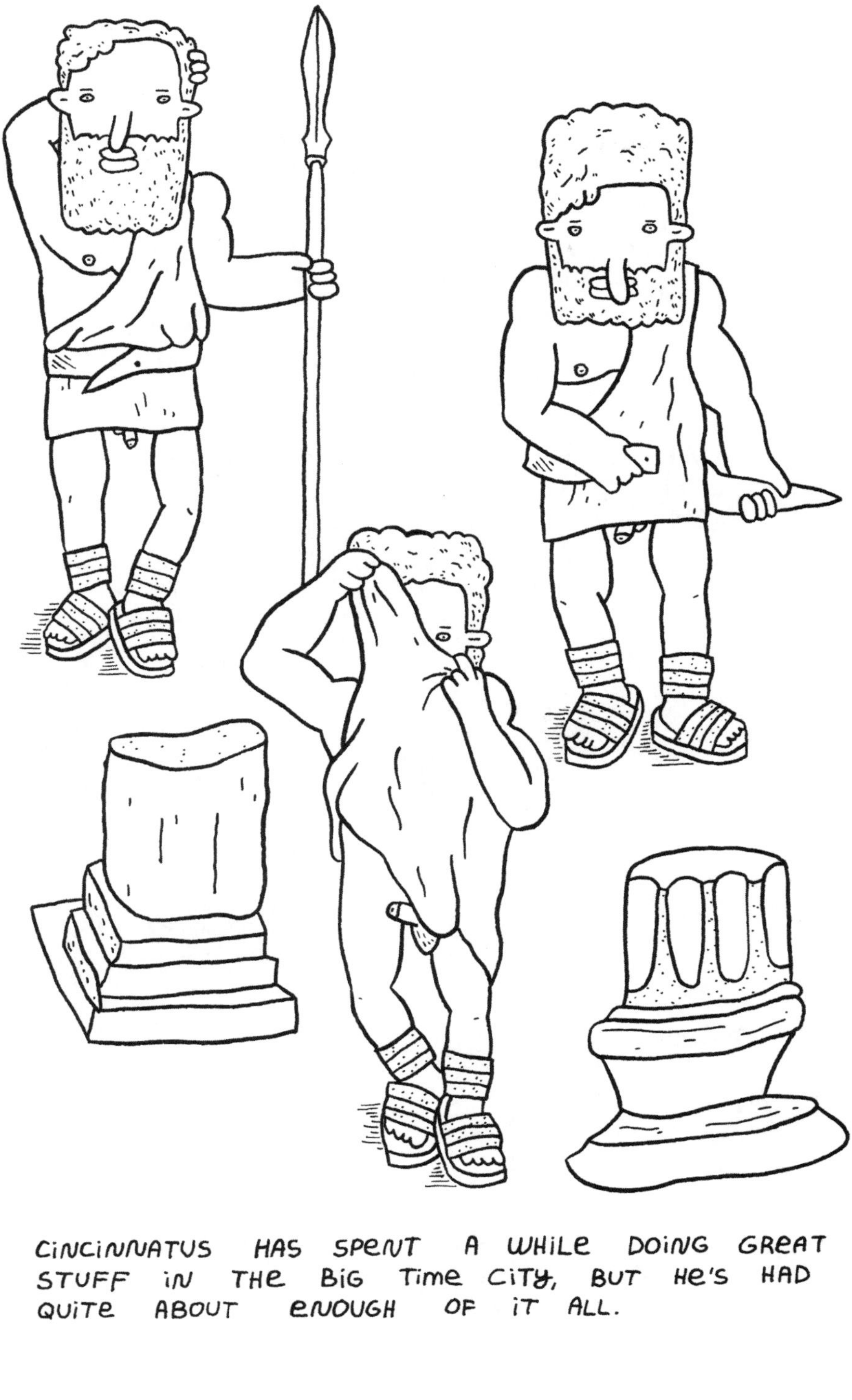

CINCINNATUS HAS SPENT A WHILE DOING GREAT STUFF IN THE BIG TIME CITY, BUT HE'S HAD QUITE ABOUT ENOUGH OF IT ALL.

SO HE PACKS UP HIS TINY APARTMENT INTO CARDBOARD BOXES AND LOADS THEM INTO THE BACK OF A RENTED CAR.

AS THOSE CINCINNATI BUILDINGS COME AROUND THE BEND, HE WHISPERS SOMETHING STUPID ABOUT THIS BEING WHERE IT'S AT.

The Contributors

David Bottoms lived in Cincinnati from 1992-2000, and while there undertook a comprehensive musical history of the city. He currently lives in Louisiana, where he is working on a book about King Records.

Cedric Michael Cox is best known for his paintings and drawings, which fall between surrealism and representational abstraction. Cox has had solo exhibits at the Contemporary Arts Center, the Carnegie Visual and Performing Arts Center, PAC Gallery, and the Aronoff Center for the Arts. His work has been featured in exhibits from Chicago to New York, as well as in two large-scale murals executed for the city of Cincinnati.

Garrett Cummins grew up in Cincinnati and started writing poetry at the age of 11. Years later, when he entered graduate school for English he focused on Composition and Rhetoric, leaving his salad days of poetry behind. He now works at the University of Cincinnati as a Composition instructor.

John Curley moved to Cincinnati from Bethesda, Maryland, in 1985 to work as a staff photographer at *The Cincinnati Enquirer*. He left *The Enquirer* in 1993 to make music full-time with The Afghan Whigs, the band he co-founded with Greg Dulli in 1986. Curley still tours with The Whigs and other bands when he's not busy running his recording studio, Ultrasuede Studio, in Camp Washington.

Aaron Delamatre is from the Show-Me State and remains terribly afraid of everything that he cannot see. After graduating from the Art Academy of Cincinnati, he managed the theater group Art & Drama Club, for which he wrote and directed five plays. He has since had exhibitions of drawings, paintings, and sculptures, constructed larger-than-life puppets, and designed several games. At any given time he has a couple of projects that he is working on, most of which lately are comic books.

Scott Devendorf plays bass in the Cincinnati-formed, Brooklyn-based band The National. He grew up in Cincinnati, where he attended the graphic design program at DAAP; he now lives in Brooklyn, New York, where he serves as creative director for the communication design studio Distant Station.

Nick Dewald is a developer/architect who runs a flea market some Saturdays and takes photos in between—more often than not, with his phone. He spent varying amounts of time paying rent in Brooklyn, Los Angeles, Chicago, and Baltimore and is pleased to be paying a mortgage in Cincinnati with his lovely wife and smiling baby. His work can be found at *nickdewald.com* or *thecityflea.com*

Maya Drozdz grew up in Gdynia, Poland and Brooklyn, New York, and has lived all over the United States. She currently resides in the historic Over-the-Rhine neighborhood in Cincinnati, where she is a founding partner of the design studio VisuaLingual. In her spare time, she wanders the streets, photographing ghost signs and other urban minutiae.

Chef David Falk, who owns and operates three restaurants as part of his Boca Restaurant Group, has lived in and honed his craft at restaurants in Chicago, Rome, and Florence. A graduate of the Culinary Institute of America, Falk moved home to Cincinnati in September 2001 and opened Boca, his first restaurant. Falk lives perched above downtown in the historic Prospect Hill neighborhood.

Rebecca Morgan Frank is the author of one collection of poems, *Little Murders Everywhere*. Her essays and profiles have appeared in *Los Angeles Review of Books*, *Black Camera*, *The Chronicle*, and *Ploughshares*. She is co-founder and editor of the online magazine Memorious and an assistant professor at the University of Southern Mississippi's Center for Writers.

Chris Glass is a designer. He likes plaid, Ke$ha, and patches.

Jack Heffron has published hundreds of magazine articles, columns, and short stories. He has written and ghostwritten nearly a dozen books, including his most recent book, *The Local Boys*, cowritten with his brother Joe. He is managing editor of manofthehouse.com and coachhub.com, a columnist for *Cincinnati Magazine*, and a journalism instructor at the University of Cincinnati.

Russell Ihrig is a comic creator and illustrator from Northern Kentucky. His comic projects include *La Petite Mort*, *Sockford*, and the forthcoming *Ectoplasm*. During the week he works as an art educator at the Cincinnati Art Museum. He received his BFA in Fine Art from The Art Academy of Cincinnati in 2003.

Polk Laffoon IV is a graduate of Yale University and the Wharton School of Business. He is a native of Cincinnati, spent most of his career with newspaper publisher Knight Ridder, where he was most recently the vice president for corporate relations. Polk does volunteer work for the Cincinnati Parks Board Foundation and the Cincinnati Art Museum, and he writes for *Cincinnati Magazine*.

Katie Laur, a bluegrass musician from Cincinnati, was born into a musical family that migrated to Detroit from the hills of Tennessee; she moved to Cincinnati in 1966. Her music has taken her from working on NPR's "Prairie Home Companion" to Russia and to the Kennedy Center. Locally, Laur hosts the radio show "Music from the Hills of Home" on WNKU and writes regularly for *Cincinnati Magazine*. She continues to work in Cincinnati to arrange shows and performances to showcase artists of a variety of styles in a variety of venues.

Sam LeCure is a relief pitcher for the Cincinnati Reds. He tweets lists of #5things he loves and appreciates about the world and Cincinnati, on season and off, as @mrLeCure on Twitter.

Zan McQuade is an editor, writer, photographer, translator, and baseball enthusiast living in Cincinnati, Ohio. Her work can be found at *zanmcquade.com*.

Linford Detweiler and **Karin Bergquist** launched Over the Rhine as a quartet in the spring of 1989, naming the ensemble after the historic, bohemian Cincinnati neighborhood Over-the-Rhine, where they lived and first wrote and recorded together. They have released thirteen studio albums, and shared the stage with such artists as Cowboy Junkies, Squeeze, John Prine, and Bob Dylan. Detweiler and Bergquist live just north of Cincinnati and perform regularly in Cincinnati and around the country.

Tifanei Ressl-Moyer is currently a law student and her favorite spot to study is in the library in the basement, third desk to the right, behind the big bookshelf. Currently, she has no hobbies, but she does well in school. Before hobby-stealing school, she traveled through Central America and Europe for two years learning new languages. Tifanei's undergraduate degree is from University of Cincinnati, where she learned that spaghetti noodles covered in chili and a mound of cheese is a very real thing.

Alex Schutte is Corporate Marketing Manager for Qvidian, a rapidly growing Boston-based software company. Alex is also on the regional board for INROADS, a national nonprofit that provides paid internships and training for talented minority youth. A Cincinnati native, he has a passion for the city and strives to be an agent of positive change for all who call this city home.

Curtis Sittenfeld is the author of the bestselling novels *Sisterland*, *American Wife*, *Prep*, and *The Man of My Dreams*. Curtis's nonfiction has appeared in many publications, including *The New York Times*, *The Atlantic Monthly*, *Salon*, *Slate*, *Glamour*, and on public radio's "This American Life." A graduate of Stanford University and the Iowa Writers' Workshop, Curtis has interviewed Michelle Obama for *Time*, appeared as a guest on NPR's "Fresh Air," and been a strangely easy "Jeopardy!" answer. Born and raised in Cincinnati, she currently resides in St. Louis.

Brian Trapp is a PhD Candidate in Comparative Literature and Fiction Writing at the University of Cincinnati, where he is the associate editor of the *Cincinnati Review*. His short stories and essays have been published in *Narrative*, *Ninth Letter*, *Black Warrior Review*, *New Ohio Review*, *The Collagist*, and *Meridian*. He is at work on a novel and a memoir. In a previous life, he worked as a newspaper journalist and taught English in China.

Jenny Ustick is a born-and-raised Cincinnatian. She creates public murals with ArtWorks, and her work (solo and collaborative) has been exhibited regionally, nationally, and internationally. She is currently a Visiting Assistant Professor at the University of Cincinnati DAAP School of Art, and currently lives on the East Side with her husband, two mutts and a cat.

Sarah Wesseler grew up in Cincinnati and now lives in Brooklyn. She is tall.

Kate Westrich is an avid hobbyist and bibliophile. She passes her time looking through a camera viewfinder, falling in love with animals, and traveling the world. You can follow her on Twitter, @KatesPOV, and on her blog, Kate's Point of View, *katespov.blogspot.com*. Kate happily lives in Cincinnati with her husband Jason and their two cats, Adagio and Notorious BIG.

Michael Wilson was born in 1959 in Cincinnati, Ohio, and has never moved away. Discovering a love of photography in college he started to make pictures in earnest and eventually began work as a freelance photographer in 1987. His work in the music industry is his most recognizable; among the artists Michael has photographed are: Lyle Lovett, B.B. King, Waylon Jennings, Randy Newman, Emmylou Harris, Bill Frisell, David Byrne, Philip Glass, Dawn Upshaw, and Doc Watson. His work can be found at *www.michaelwilsonphotographer.com.*

"Geology is Destiny" by Polk Laffoon IV previously appeared in the May 2012 issue of *Cincinnati Magazine*. Printed by permission of the author and *Cincinnati Magazine.*

"Love Letter to Cincinnati" by David Falk previously appeared in *The Huffington Post* on October 23, 2013. Printed by permission of the author.

"Over-The-Rhine" by Sarah Wesseler previously appeared in *Satellite Magazine.* Printed by permission of the author and *Satellite Magazine.*

"My City in Two Dog Parks" by Brian Trapp previously appeared in the Fall/ Winter 2012 issue of *Black Warrior Review*. Printed by permission of the author and *Black Warrior Review.*

"Pushing the Racial Dialogue in Cincinnati" by Tifanei Ressl-Moyer previously appeared on *UrbanCincy.com* in February 2011. Printed by permission of the author and *UrbanCincy.com.*

"Freestore Foodbank" by Curtis Sittenfeld previously appeared in the October 2007 issue of *Cincinnati Magazine*. Printed by permission of the author and *Cincinnati Magazine.*

"Pete Rose" by Jack Heffron previously appeared in the October 2007 issue of *Cincinnati Magazine.* Printed by permission of the author and *Cincinnati Magazine.*

"Growing Up Half-Black in Cincinnati" by Alex Schutte previously appeared on *UrbanCincy.com* in February 2011. Printed by permission of the author and *UrbanCincy.com.*

"Conversations with Irma" by Katie Laur previously appeared in the September 1993 issue of *Cincinnati Magazine*. Printed by permission of the author and *Cincinnati Magazine.*

"Called Home" lyrics from the 2012 album *Meet Me At The Edge Of The World,* published by Great Speckled Dog Records. Printed by permission of Over The Rhine.